CHRISTIAN'S WAY

BY

Christie Maajoun

This book is dedicated to Christian Maajoun.

*Thank you for changing my life,
for being my Holland.*

Welcome to Holland

By Emily Perl Kingsley

When you're going to have a baby, it's like planning a fabulous vacation trip - to Italy. You buy a bunch of guide books and make your wonderful plans. The Coliseum. The Michelangelo David. The gondolas in Venice. You may learn some handy phrases in Italian. It's all very exciting.

After months of eager anticipation, the day finally arrives. You pack your bags and off you go. Several hours later, the plane lands. The stewardess comes in and says, "Welcome to Holland."

"Holland?!?" you say. "What do you mean Holland?? I signed up for Italy! I'm supposed to be in Italy. All my life I've dreamed of going to Italy."

But there's been a change in the flight plan. They've landed in Holland and there you must stay.

The important thing is that they haven't taken you to a horrible, disgusting, filthy place, full of pestilence, famine and disease. It's just a different place.

So, you must go out and buy new guide books. And you must learn a whole new language. And you will meet a whole new group of people you would never have met.

It's just a different place. It's slower-paced than Italy, less flashy than Italy. But after you've been there for a while and you catch your breath, you look around.... and you begin to notice that Holland has windmills....and Holland has tulips. Holland even has Rembrandts.

But everyone you know is busy coming and going from Italy... and they're all bragging about what a wonderful time they had there. And for the rest of your life, you will say "Yes, that's where I was supposed to go. That's what I had planned."

And the pain of that will never, ever, ever, ever go away... because the loss of that dream is a very, very, significant loss.

But... if you spend your life mourning the fact that you didn't get to Italy, you may never be free to enjoy the very special, the very lovely things ... about Holland.

Introduction

Did you know a fan powers a water fountain?

My son Christian and I were walking in a park, hand in hand, when he spotted a water fountain. On an impulse, he released my hand and ran over to it. I stayed where he left me, giving him space as he examined it from different angles. Then he got on his left knee and touched it, not as a little boy would touch anything, but more like a horse-whisperer would gently touch a mare, tenderly, with exploratory fingers, as if needing to understand it.

Then he smiled. "Mom, there's a fan in here!"

I found out later, when I Google'd it, that he was right! By just looking and touching the fountain, he deduced something most people in the world never would have. However, my son doesn't possess super-hero or mystical powers. He can't see through iron, walls, or fountains. In fact, the world has even decided that my son isn't even your typical child, that he's less than your average child. So how did this tender little boy know there was a fan that powered the water fountain?

My son's senses are heightened. Christian has Autism.

I wrote this book because when I first found out that my son was autistic, even though there are seemingly millions of blogs or articles on autism and bookstores are widening shelf space for books on autism, I couldn't find the information I was looking for and that led me to bouts of despair, denial, and rage.

I had so many questions. I didn't know if his diagnosis would soon be followed by his death. I didn't know how my daughter, his older sister, was going to react to it. I didn't know how my loving but busy-with-his-job-to-take-care-of-the-financial-needs-of-our-family husband was going to cope with it. Especially with Christian being his only son.

I was lost. I was in pain. I questioned everything in my life. Had God abandoned me or did He never exist after all? *Is this my fault? Will my son be ridiculed his entire life? How much strain will it bring to our family dynamic?* What did other parents do? What was I supposed to do with him when he got to high school? *Will he ever have a girlfriend? Is he going to live with us for the rest of his life?*

My entire world had imploded, but all I could do was send silent screams out to the universe. I talked to myself in third person; "You're a mother. Your kids need you. You need to be strong."

So, I became strong. I became knowledgeable. I evolved from a loving mother to a loving mother who is also the primary caretaker of a child with a disability, who also made sure that her other child, her only daughter, had everything she needed, who also was there to be a loving and supportive wife to a charming, ultra-positive husband. That's a whole different species of mother.

In this book, I hope you will find the hope you desperately need, even if you don't think you do. I asked other mothers of children with autism to share their stories, too, so that this book would cater to your journey, regardless of what age your child is.

But at its core, this book is for the parents of an autistic child of between two and six years of age. My heart goes out to you because I know what you're going through. You are so hurt that the English language is not equipped to properly express the jumbled emotions you're feeling. But I'm here to tell you… there's a light at the end of the tunnel.

There is a joy your child will give you unlike anything else you've ever experienced. There is a new depth to you, never seen before by anyone, including you, that can engulf the raw emotions that are eating you up and keeping you awake at night. You'll have to read this book to find out what that depth is, but trust me, when you do, everything will click for you.

What is Unconditional Love?

I've heard those words strung together at school, at lunch, at church. But it's something I never felt I had. I don't believe most people understand the concept. I think that at the center of our minds, we're all, even the noblest among us, selfish and pretty self-serving.

My friend, and a great relationship coach,

Joel Clemons says this about unconditional love: *"Unconditional love is loving someone without conditions. It's not making your love for someone dependent on what you receive from them. It's loving without limits or expectations. Unconditional love is the willingness to put aside how you feel in order to fully be open, available and present for someone else. It's the free gift that you give someone because their happiness is your happiness."*

To love unconditionally, wow, that's beyond impressive; it's really tough to do. Yet, I do have unconditional love in my heart. Christian gave it to me.

I held nothing back on the telling of my story. I hope I don't come across as I am at times; selfish, egotistical, vain, or resentful. If I do, I hope you appreciate my openness. But at the end of the day, this book is not about me. It's not even about Christian. It's about you and your child. This book is to help you understand what to expect tomorrow and the years to come after.

Just do me one favor, the next time you see a water fountain, remember that Christian, my autistic little boy, taught you that a fan powers it. Then smile, because everything is going to be all right.

Autism

A neurodevelopmental disorder characterized by impaired social interaction, verbal and non-verbal communication, and restricted and repetitive behavior.

Autism Spectrum Disorder Frequency

In 2012, 1 out of 68 children were diagnosed with Autism Spectrum Disorder according to estimates from the Center for Disease Control. According to Autism Speaks, a respected autism advocacy organization, the most recent National Health Interview Survey suggests numbers as high as 1 in 45 children.

Table of Contents

Welcome to Holland, By Emily Perl Kingsley 3
Introduction 5
PART I 13
Chapter 1: You Didn't Ask for This 15
Chapter 2: Once Upon a Time 21
Chapter 3: A Mother Knows 27
Chapter 4: Hope found in the oddest place 39
CHAPTER 5: My Life Had Changed 43
Chapter 6: Life is unfair 49
Chapter 7: Our New Normal 53
Chapter 8: A Father's Perspective,
by George Maajoun 63
PART II 71
Chapter 9: The Power of Love, by Angela
Cochran 73
Chapter 10: Faith Triumphs the Dark Ages,
by Martha Martin 81
Chapter 11: One World, by Riffat Merchant 97
Chapter 12: Early Detection,
by Katheryn Luker 107
Chapter 13: When Challenges Happen,
by Melissa Mottern 117

Chapter 14: The Flutie Foundation,
by Lisa Borges 123

Chapter 15: Dr. Springer Shares His Thoughts,
by Dr. George Springer 131

PART III 141

Chapter: 16: Early and Late Signs of Autism.. 143

Chapter 17: My Action Plan for Parents 149

Chapter 18: It Really Does Take a Village 155

Chapter 19: My Vision for Christian 161

Chapter 20: I'm Just a Caring Mom Trying
to Help 163

Acknowledgments 169

About the Author 173

PART I

CHAPTER 1

You Didn't Ask for This

"I find the best way to love someone is not to change them, but instead, help them reveal the greatest version of themselves." Steve Maraboli

    First and foremost, I want to let you know that you're not alone. I know you didn't ask for this. No one does. It's a full-time job today to consistently be content and happy while striving to live a better life day after day. Life throws us enough curve balls that derail us from our goals and dreams. It seems unfair to throw this into the mix.

    You didn't ask for your child to be born autistic. You never thought your parenting love and skills would be pushed past what you thought were its limits. But here you are, probably shocked or feeling an emotion that will sooner or later turn into anger. Angry because it just isn't fair. Now, what the hell do you do? I felt the same way.

All I wanted was the basics; a great life with a great husband and great kids and making great money and going on great vacations and laughing a great deal. Was that too much to ask for? I'm not sure if it was or not but that's not what I got, well not entirely.

To be truthful, I got some of the things I had always wanted; I have a great husband, I have great kids, there were times in my adult life when we made great money, and I have laughed a great deal. However, just because things look good on paper, it doesn't mean it tells the whole story. Kind of like someone's "great life" on Facebook, it doesn't tell the whole story. We don't post pictures or videos of the times we cry, the times we worry, the times we've failed, and the times we wished we could have a redo. But this is life…. and mine, well, I didn't ask for what I got.

I too didn't ask to be a mother of an autistic child.

I had my suspicions that something was amiss but I didn't dare to believe that my son wasn't typical. When Christian was diagnosed with Autism, the world fell out from under my feet, and it took me years to find solid footing again.

An untold number of parents have gone through what I'm going through, and many more will in upcoming years. That's why I wrote this book, to impart with them the knowledge I've gained when I spent thousands of hours researching (obsessing) on how to best care for my child.

There is so much information on the web. There are a lot of truths, a lot of half-truths, and a lot of false information out there. I'll say it; a lot of crap, there's a ton of crap out there. I almost went insane believing some of the crap I read about autism and trying to deal with the mental and physical state of my son. I first experienced indignant denial, "There's nothing wrong with my son!" Then I fell into a deep depression when I didn't want to see anyone, speak to anyone or hear from anyone. In particular, friends who were parents of typical children. Oooh, I was pretty vicious during that time.... vicious to myself.

I want to make sure you're not beating yourself up. It's not your fault. You aren't broken internally. You don't require fixing. Too many parents in these situations drive themselves crazy thinking about what they could have done differently. If their first child was born autistic, they wonder if the rest of their children will be as well.

Breathe. Inhale... exhale... inhale... exhale...

It's not your fault.

Save your strength. You need to get ready for what's coming. I want you to understand the steps you might need to go through and the myriad emotions you'll probably go through. I'm here to give you some insight to help you to get through some things you didn't expect.

The way you view your life, your perspective, will determine your reality. If you are going to cry,

"Woe is me" all day, every day, you're going to live a miserable life. You will not be able to properly, with the right attitude, help your child reach his or her potential. This means you're going to have to be mentally stronger than you ever have been before.

I want you to know this...this is important: some blessings come in disguise. You may feel you've been dealt a crappy hand, but that's what life dealt you. You didn't have a choice. What you do have a choice in is determining how you are going to play the hand you've been dealt. Your life isn't over. Your child's life isn't over either; it just started.

Window of opportunity

Your child's early or "formative" years are absolutely critical. There is a difference of opinion as to how big or small the window of opportunity is. Some people say it's between 3-6 and others, like Laurie Stephens, Ph.D. say it's between 0-6. While there is a varying degree of when this window opens, most scholars and doctors of the topic tend to agree it closes at around six years of age.

In other words, you don't have time to mope around feeling sorry for yourself; the clock is ticking! Before the ripe old age of six, the brain still has a high degree of plasticity, which means it is still being shaped or molded. It's time to get some Early Intervention (EI) going.

In a published paper by Dr. Stephens called "Early Intervention in Autism: Forging the Architecture for

Chang," Dr. Stephens writes, "Statistics show that between 25 and 50% of children receiving intensive Early Intervention will move into general education by Kindergarten. Many others will need significantly less service provision in future years."

It's imperative to know how to parent your child during this time. Parenting your child might require more than teaching manners and a consistent bedtime. Special attention might have to be paid to diet and gestures, since your child might be slow to develop speech and a prolonged state of diaper usage.

Some people grieve for their children when they are diagnosed with Autism. Please, pay attention. Your child has not passed away. Nothing is over. You are not alone. The Autistic community opens its arms to welcome your family with a loving and knowing embrace.

I welcome you, too. Therein lies the reason for this book.

Please, I invite you to read my story. Read other people's stories in the middle section of this book. Our stories will help you.

We promise.

Chapter 2

Once Upon a Time

"...and she loved a little boy very, very, much, even more than she loved herself."
Shel Silverstein

For most women, finding out we are expecting a baby is one of our happiest moments. Before long, we hear praises for our glow and get smiles and well wishes from friends and strangers alike. Many of us indulge our cravings and, my favorite part, eat as much of those as we can.

Not only do Moms' lives change, so do the lives of those closest to us. Newborns affect the family months before they are born. But all is well the day Baby finally arrives! OMG, what is better than that?

Unfortunately, not every child is born healthy. Some families can't just add that one little person and move on. Today, 1 out of 68 children are diagnosed with Autism Spectrum Disorder, a diagnosis that includes many different conditions.

For most people, lives change for the better when a new child enters the home. For others, including parents of a child with Autism Spectrum Disorder (ASD), their lives change in ways they never imagined.

A Little About Me

When I was a little girl, I dreamed of becoming a princess. Most girls did at that time and still do today. However, with the empowerment of women and all of society depicting more independent, goal-oriented and determined women, little girls today also dream of being superheroes, astronauts, or powerful political figures. Not all women get to live out their dreams; I am one of the lucky ones who did.

Did I become a princess? Yes, the day my prince charming asked me to marry him. He proposed and, of course, I said yes! (I might have actually screamed, yes). We owned a thriving gas station that housed a Subway adjacent to a carwash. For all intents and purposes, we were pretty well set. I was living my fairytale life. Our wedding had been perfect and remains one of my treasured memories.

Although our business expenses were high, the income more than covered everything. My husband George had his loyal steed, Lamborghini, and I had my little castles (rental houses) that I managed. We were a strong team. Life was better than good; it was better than great. My life was the fulfillment of my dreams.

A year into our marriage, we decided to try and

have a child. We were ready to share our kingdom with a royal baby. Our good fortune continued, and soon we were expecting! I wanted a boy---you know, the classic heir to the throne, but we found out our first child would be a girl. I was fine with that; I knew decorating a baby girl's nursery—and Baby girl would be more fun and frillier. I went all out to prepare the way for the world's next princess.

However, maybe there is no such thing as 'Happily Ever After' because life is a constant onslaught of changes and adapting. Our lives changed when business competition showed up; someone opened a gas station right next to ours. Subsequently, they took half of our business. The fairy tale was trembling. We had trouble paying the $21,000 a month rent and eventually lost the business. Then the recession hit our area in 2007, and, financially, we spiraled downward. We lost our houses and had to give up our expensive cars. However, all was not lost...I was still carrying our little princess.

On April 11, 2007, Brianna Jean Maajoun was born. I was able to have a natural birth, with a little help from an epidural. It was a magical moment; George was in the room to greet his daughter, and our parents waited outside the room anxious to see the new addition to the family. We were incredibly proud. Brianna had a lot of hair and looked healthy and fit. My father was a body builder, and George and I enjoyed an active lifestyle. She definitely had our genes.

Brianna was a great baby. However, in the

beginning, she was colicky. We walked the floor with her every evening, frustrated with her crying. There wasn't much we could do to give her or us relief until we finally found a formula that helped calm her stomach and ease her pain. Before long the colic ceased.

We had cleared our first big parenting hurdle. Financially, we had to start over, but we were ready. I went from buying whatever to selling Avon. I wanted to help provide for the new princess.

Life in the Maajoun household stabilized and was getting better. I had adjusted to the life of mothering. George was out being a great provider – always looking for ways to improve our living conditions, and Brianna was a normal, active, inquisitive, and charming toddler. Life was easy-peasy. After Brianna turned two, George and I began to try to have another child. We really wanted that boy. However, it didn't appear to be in the cards for us.

After three years of being unsuccessful at getting pregnant, I began to lose hope that it would happen again. I went back to work as a teacher. I had a few students with autism and other disabilities and remember thinking, please God, don't test me with a child like this. A couple of years after that, I experienced a horrible pain on my right side. The sonogram showed that a huge cyst was the culprit. Three weeks after it had ruptured on its own, I conceived again. This time it was a boy!

I was just as active during my second pregnancy as I had been in my first. I worked out at the gym and made sure I ate well. Working with kids with disabilities pushed me to research what types of things I should do and what types of foods I should or shouldn't eat to have the healthiest boy possible. I gave up eating cold cuts when I learned they harbor listeria, a bacteria which pregnant women are more likely to be affected by that can cause harm to developing babies. Some women might have taken the chance, but not me! I did everything I could to avoid exposure to toxins.

When I was eleven weeks into my pregnancy, I started to bleed and was rushed to the hospital. I had been over-exerting myself and was told I needed bed rest. I was a terrible patient, however, since I was accustomed to always 'doing' something. So, my husband and parents arranged to take me to a secluded area where I would be forced to rest. They took me to a cabin in the woods near Rainbow River. I did what I was told; I stayed in bed. Although it was one of the toughest things I'd faced yet, my body got back to where it was supposed to be.

That pregnancy brought with it other challenges. George went to California for six months to start a new business venture with a family member. For the most part, I was all alone taking care of a 4-year-old girl, working as a teacher, keeping up with the house, paying the bills and doing everything else that needed to be done, all while I was pregnant. During a routine checkup, I was told that I was low on B12 and needed a shot. Before taking the shot, the nurse told me, "I just want you to know before you take this shot that it's been linked to Autism." I refused the shot. I did not want God to test me with a child that had any type of disability.

The date was March 19, 2012, when our son was born. George had made it in time to see his son come into the world. When the nurse asked me for his name, I was ecstatic. I had picked out my son's name ten years before and was elated to officially announce, "His name is Christian George Maajoun." Our family was complete, and I was very happy.

The fairy tale was making a comeback.

Chapter 3

A Mother Knows

"My children taught me the true meaning of unconditional love."
Yvonne Pierre

My little boy was every mother's dream, a perfect, handsome, little angel. He barely made a peep unless he was hungry or needed a diaper change. Compared to my spitfire daughter and her early months, he was easy peasy.

When he was about four months old, I began to sense something was different. I couldn't quite put my finger on it, but my mother's intuition was nudging at the back of my mind.

Christian would sit in his baby seat and stare at the ceiling fan, in his own little world, completely mesmerized. For his first Christmas, at 8-months-old, I bought him his own little fan. I thought it was so cute how intrigued he was with fans, yet something about it didn't seem quite normal. When I mentioned it to people, they would just shrug, "Eh, all kids like fans." And that is true.

A gnawing fear kept tugging at me, but it was as if I refused to see what it wanted me to see. After talking to myself at length about it, I finally brought it up to George. "Honey, I'm worried. Something is off with Christian."

George, a strong, Lebanese man didn't appear to want to engage in any talk about something being wrong. When he would play and talk with Christian, he would tell him how they would play sports together and do other manly things.

One day, I told George, "Have you noticed how Christian chokes when he eats? Sometimes it looks like he's about to have, or having a seizure."

"Sweetheart, if you're concerned, take him to the doctor, have it checked out."

I took him for a checkup at ten-months, and the doctor couldn't find anything and just told me to "keep an eye on it."

So that's what I did. I watched everything Christian did. My intuition was slowly getting louder, telling me something wasn't right. I would fight it whenever I would see Christian laugh or do something that all infants do, but it wouldn't go away. So, I continued to watch him, and pray.

He had quirky little habits. At first, I would think it was cute, but then the worry would set in. He went through a stage where he would shrug his shoulder up and down repeatedly. Right when I was ready to talk to the doctor about it, he grew out of it. Maybe it's not such a big deal. But the uneasy feeling grew, and I couldn't shake it.

He continued to grow and started walking, albeit a little later than most kids. He was constantly walking on his tiptoes. If he wasn't walking, he was spinning. He would put his right hand in front of him and stare at it to keep from getting dizzy as he would spin in circles for hours and hours. Again, I mentioned my concerns and people responded, "Oh, boys like to spin," with a chuckle. I only had experience with a girl, so I allowed myself to believe other people.

I couldn't wait for his regularly scheduled checkup. I breathed a sigh of relief when the doctor told me he was fine. "Thank you, God," I said softly as I drove home. But in my heart, I just knew, *something is different about my son.*

Before Christian was born, Brianna was an only child, and yeah, she was a little spoiled. Let's just say she was used to getting whatever her little heart desired. My concerns for Christian took too much attention away from my daughter and changed my relationship with her. It was hard on all of us, but her daddy and I did all we could to give her the love she needed. Christian was still a baby, barely into the toddler stage, and he needed me in a way she didn't. Brianna became Daddy's girl.

I was so focused on Christian. I couldn't stop wondering why I had that worrisome feeling. *Is he a genius? I don't know; I just know he's different.*

As my friend Nancy and I sat on the patio sipping ice tea and chatting, Christian tippy-toed by, and the feeling struck again. I leaned toward my girlfriend, and, for the first time ever, said what had been bothering me. "I think he might have autism." I had finally put a name to the riddle that had been eluding me.

She sputtered out her tea and looked at me like I'd lost my mind. "Shut up! Girl, you are out of control. That boy is just fine!"

I wanted to believe it; I wanted to blindly accept all the blithe reassurances of my husband, my doctor, my family, and friends. But I just couldn't! I knew, only in the way a mother can that something was wrong with my little boy.

I could see that Christian had a high sensitivity to most things, and at other times it seemed he would seek danger. He scared the daylights out of me when he climbed the highest place he could find. Before I was watching him every moment to see signs of something, anything, but then I couldn't dare take my eyes off him for fear he would hurt himself. Something was always going in his mouth: sticks, all sorts of stuff. He chewed everything in sight. He would grind his teeth and rub his tongue on the back of his teeth. At first, I thought it was just teething, but no... I knew it was something more.

I was researching like a madwoman, determined to find a solution for my son, for myself, for my family. I was overwhelmed by the many heartbreaking stories I found on the internet, and there were moments when I felt like I couldn't breathe. I knew there was a solution, a way to make him whole, but I just couldn't find it. All the while, Christian slipped developmentally a little more each day.

I was getting so much information, and my emotions were running amuck with me to the point that I got serious with my journal, writing in it everything I found and every feeling of anxiety and depression I felt.

On May 7, 2014, Christian went to his first occupational therapy evaluation which revealed he needed therapy to help regulate his senses.

"Your son has symptoms that indicate he may have a sensory processing disorder. Occupational therapy can help children with sensory issues to function at a more developmentally appropriate level," the therapist explained. "We'd also like to place him on the waiting list for speech."

I was willing to do whatever needed to be done to help him. I signed him up, and the therapy began; two times a week, thirty minutes each session.

The next day, May 8, 2014, Christian had his first neurology evaluation. I bit my nails as an EEG was performed, and breathed a sigh of relief when the neurologist informed, "The EEG is normal." But the evaluation didn't stop there.

He received a diagnosis of PDD (Pervasive Developmental Disorder). The neurologist patiently explained, "This is a disorder found on the lower side of the Autism spectrum. Children with this disorder often have the type of difficulties you've shared with me concerning Christian but are not considered to be autistic; they just have some autistic tendencies."

"So, where do I go from here? What can I do to help Christian?" I was feeling desperate, and it showed, but I didn't care. I needed answers!

"Unfortunately, there's not much more we can do. Continue with his therapy and see what happens from there. Children with PDD are not eligible for any further services."

I left the appointment and walked to my car with my mind running a mile a minute. As I drove home, with Christian buckled in a car seat behind me, I was assaulted with memories.

- Christian shuddering at 4-months-old
- Christian staring at a ceiling fan and not responding to his name
- Christian tippy-toeing through the house
- Christian spinning and spinning
- Christian chewing on dangerous objects
- Christian climbing to the top of the kitchen cabinets
- Me saying, "I love you," to my little boy and receiving no response, not even eye contact

On May 9, I could do nothing but cry!

At the Park

May 10 was a bittersweet day. We went to the park, George, Brianna, Christian and I. George and I sat on a bench watching the children play. I looked over at him, wanting to connect and enjoy the moment, but instead, I saw heartbreak in his eyes. George had the expression on his face that I had come to know as sadness. I touched his arm, nearly speechless, "Honey?"

He turned his head slowly to look at me. I could see the moisture gathering in his eyes. His voice cracked with grief. "It just dawned on me. Christian may never play soccer." In that one sentence, he summed up to me that all his hopes and dreams for his first son and only son were dashed. His admission of defeat hit both of us like a ton of bricks. He turned away and hung his head. I moved closer and curled into his side.

"George, I'm afraid. Please promise you'll never leave. Our family is really going to need you, more than we ever have before."

"Honestly, babe, I wish you wouldn't have opened my eyes to the things you've noticed, I'm starting to worry, what if you're right. I wish I could go back to believing Christian was just a normal little boy, if only for a little while longer. It's hard to enjoy him growing up when I'm afraid for his future."

I nodded and gave him a half-smile. I felt I had robbed him of happy months with Christian when he was an infant. George probably would have never noticed the things I had. Now it was too late, the prognosis declared. I wished I could've gone back in time and let him enjoy those months in bliss, but I couldn't. He put a strong arm around me and pulled me close. For a moment, I felt safe from the storm.

Christian was the sweetest little 2-year-old. He lived in two worlds; one was his own and the other craved touch – physical contact and love. He invited me to join him by gesturing with his tiny arm and often did the same with Daddy and Sissy. When we responded in a way he didn't like, he would point at his little nose. We realized this was his way of saying no. We animated our speech whenever we spoke to him and, when we were lucky, we were rewarded with a giggle.

We hoped and prayed he would grow out of PDD. We no longer shared our situation with anyone; it was just too painful. I needed a safe place to express the wide range of feelings I was experiencing and poured everything into my journal.

I had survived one of the worst weeks of my life.

The summer was an emotional roller coaster filled with therapy sessions and doctor's appointments. I was doing everything I possibly could to help my son, but when I looked at my daughter, I was overwhelmed with guilt. I felt like I was neglecting her in the worst way, and it broke my heart.

I decided I needed to do something about it and give her something that was just for her. George's cousin, affectionately known as Cham, had asked me if I wanted a bunny. So, knowing that I could give it back if I had to, I agreed to it and BAM, we had two bunnies! Brianna was so excited, until we came home and found one of the bunnies was dead. Her devastation didn't last when I offered to buy a new bunny.

So off we went to the pet store to replace the bunny. Little did we know, but our bunny adventures were just beginning. Our next surprise was to find that a squirrel had gotten into the screened-in patio and was terrifying the bunnies, trying to chew his way into their cage. Have you ever heard a bunny cry? It is the worst high-pitched whine you'll ever hear in your life.

With bunnies screaming in the background, I called pest control and found out the best way to get squirrels out is to lure them with a very specific treat. I leaned over the cage, with Brianna close by, enlarged the hole the squirrel had made and held out a cracker slathered in peanut butter. Much to my relief, it worked and the squirrel left. Another brave mommy moment that will probably never be appreciated.

I continued to keep myself busy with appointments, researching, and journaling; I survived one day at a time by continually looking for an answer. There were many nights I fell into bed completely exhausted and cried myself to sleep as I worried over my little boy's future.

My intuition was confirmed on September 3, 2014.

We finally had our visit with Dr. Mary Pavan, a neurodevelopmental specialist who worked with Early Steps. After examining Christian and performing assessments, the doctor informed George and me that she would contact us with the results.

I was shocked that she wasn't going to give us a diagnosis, and I couldn't wait another minute. "Does our son have autism?" I bluntly asked.

The doctor looked me in the eye, "Are you certain you want my diagnosis today?"

I didn't flinch. "That's why we're here. We want to get him all the help he needs. So, yes. Absolutely, yes."

I half expected her to say no. "Yes, I believe he does," she said. I don't think I could ever properly explain what I felt at that moment. It was as if a cold pain had started somewhere deep in my stomach and slowly spread through my entire body. I was sure my heart would want to stop once the coldness touched it. My eardrums did a vibration foreign to me, and all other sound was suspended, except for the sound of my quickening, pounding heart. I think that's the exact same feeling I would've felt if she had given me a death sentence. My world crumbled around me.

Yet, I wouldn't cry. I didn't gasp. I wanted this whole scene to be wrong; I wanted that cold feeling to be wrong; I wanted all of this to go away. I wished I hadn't wanted an answer so badly. I wished we weren't sitting there.

The next few moments were a blur. I could hear the doctor giving us information, and a nurse came in to tell us about support groups. Everyone tried to give us their best 'encouraging' look, but all I could do was stare back blankly, barely able to register anything.

I wasn't ready to face this, and it was obvious George wasn't ready either. With Christian in his arms, George hurried outside. And suddenly I felt lost and alone, completely lost, completely alone.

Chapter 4

Hope found in the oddest place

"The moment we began treating Asperger's as one of our greatest gifts was the moment everything changed for the better." Asperger Experts

We rode home in silence. To call it uncomfortable silence would not do justice to the way the heavy mood in the car was. When we got home, I couldn't go inside. "I'm going to Publix," I said as I walked from the passenger side of the car to the driver's side. I don't recall if George said something or even looked at me. I needed to be alone.

I got to the grocery store and picked up the items I needed in a daze. As the cashier finished ringing up the items, the young man who was bagging my groceries smiled at me and asked how my day was going.

I tried to match his cheery smile, but I'm sure I gave him a sad one. "It could be better."

He put the final bag in my cart as I slid my debit card through the machine. "What would make today be the best day of your life?"

I didn't know how to answer. Before I could stop myself, I said, "For God to take away my son's autism." I don't know what I expected, probably some consolation. But what happened next shocked me.

"Why?" he asked. It seemed like the worst question. I really looked at him, focused on him for the first time. His little question snapped me out of my daze. "I have autism," he said. "Asperger's."

The way he said it, so nonchalantly, as if it was no big deal, impacted my heart in a way I can't describe. "Let me help you with your groceries; I'll walk you to the car." With a smile, he got behind the cart and walked alongside me.

He began to talk about himself. My life hung on every word. He told me that he was working at Publix part-time while he was attending a popular trade school to become a mechanic. "I love working on cars," he said.

He put the groceries in my car and opened the door for me. I didn't know if I should cry for him, hug him, or be happy for him. He certainly did not fit the mold of what I thought someone with autism was. When I sat back down, he shut my door like a perfect gentleman.

What just happened? I drove home on auto-pilot.

Once groceries were unloaded, I felt mentally in need of the gym. "I'm leaving," I called out and rushed to the car.

Parked in front, I sent out a text to my immediate family about receiving Christian's diagnosis. There was no way I was ready to talk to anyone about it. "Just found out Christian's diagnosis, he has autism. Will talk later, but please not today." I was optimistic in the text. I told them he could lose the diagnosis by age 5. The family understood and was very supportive. With that taken care of, I walked into the gym.

After signing in, I went to class, got my equipment set up and tried to focus on my workout. I needed routine, a routine I felt was going to get drastically changed.

I showed the text to Brian Lee, my trainer. He hugged me. High-Intensity Interval Training with Brain was about to start when my friend Renee arrived. I hugged her then the flood of tears blocked my phone's text from my view when I held it out for her to read.

I started Mountain Climbing, the first part of Interval Training, with red, swollen eyes and a streaked face. I reminded myself to breathe. At that moment I thought to myself, you have to be strong. *You have no choice but to be strong---strong for everything and everyone in your life.*

CHAPTER 5

My Life Had Changed

"Being a mother is learning about strengths you didn't know you had, and dealing with fears you didn't know existed." Linda Wooten

When I finally got settled at home, I knew my life had changed. I didn't know how much or even if I could handle it. Scenes of little Christian kept playing in the carousel of my mind. At first those scenes seemed innocent enough. However, as they played over and over, I could see the dreaded disease that had been with him for... how long? I saw, but in no way accepted; my heart was present, but my brain had gone AWOL.

I pushed back all questions I had no answers for:

- How did this happen to Christian?
- Will he be able to go to a regular school?

- Is he a prime target for bullies?
- Do I need to be available 24/7?
- Will I be able to work outside the home?
- How will George handle this?
- Will Brianna feel left out if Christian needs all our attention?
- Will other mothers look at me funny, as if it's my fault?
- Is this my fault?
- Could I have prevented this?
- Is there a cure?
- What am I supposed to do next?

    I wanted to talk to other people about how I was feeling, but I was battling way too many emotions to talk rationally to anyone. I was incredibly sad for Christian; I was embarrassed for our family, and I was angry at how unfair this was to us...to me...to him!

    Days later, I followed our pediatrician's direction and took Christian to his first scheduled therapy session. The session scared the daylights out of me. The waiting room at the doctor visits I had experienced up to that point all housed typical children. Children waiting to be seen played with the toys they had brought, colored in coloring books, played with mobile devices, and behaved. I was not expecting to see what I saw when I opened the door to the therapy doctor's office; it was one of the saddest sites I ever saw.

In the waiting room were parents with solemn expressions and children who looked defeated. Most of the children had some visible disabilities. I didn't know if the kids were medicated, but it sure looked that way. There was such a heavy presence in that room that I wanted to grab my son and run out. I smiled tightly at the only parent who looked up to see who had entered the room and then checked in at the counter at the far end of the room.

Thankfully, there were enough open seats that I didn't have to sit right next to anyone. Christian sat next to me, staring at the other kids, a loud bunch if I ever saw one. I guess he was only used to being with his sister and family members. I followed his gaze and realized that he was staring at a girl with pretty, blond curls who looked to be a couple of years older than he was. She wore blue jeans and a lemon-yellow shirt. On the bottom of the shirt was a little hole that had the little girl transfixed. She would put her right index finger in the hole and twirl the bottom of her shirt around. Then she would take her right finger out, put her left index finger in the hole, and do the same. She kept switching from finger to finger, and Christian kept staring. My daughter and I have dark hair so to this day I'm not sure if he was looking at her because of her blond curls or if he, too, was transfixed by the little hole in her shirt. He finally stopped staring at her after they called her name and her mother guided her out of the waiting room and into the doctor's hallway.

That's when I noticed a man in about his early 40's in dress pants, shoes, and a dress shirt looking hard at Christian. I felt that he was trying to determine what flaw my child had. I squeezed Christian's right arm as if to give him confidence, but honestly, I think Christian was okay. I was the one having the tough time. I looked at the other kids and couldn't help but wonder what was wrong with each of them. I'm usually a chatty, friendly person. If you're going to be in my close proximity for any length of time, I'll start chatting you up. However, that room was so glum and quiet that I didn't say a word.

Then, as if on an invisible queue, the children started getting loud. It began with one of them banging a plastic Spiderman action figure on the metal part of the fold-up chairs we sat on. The effect of that banging was amazing. With a few seconds of banging, the other children seemed to wake up from their delirium. One girl who appeared to have Down syndrome started to wail as if she were trying to sing a song but forgot the words and the notes. Another child, a boy, took off his sandals and started to bang his head against the wall. I was flabbergasted.

God, why did you allow this to happen to all these kids? What did their families do to deserve this? Or are you not real? I looked at Christian, who had started flying his toy plane over his head, oblivious to what anyone else was doing. I didn't feel pity for him. All I felt was the love of a mother. *They say, Lord, You won't give us anything we can't handle. Please help me handle this.* Still, I wanted to walk out. *I was out of place. I don't belong here!*

"Christian? Christian Ma - Maaj...Christian?"

I smirked as I stood up. No one could ever read our last name right. "Maajoun," (may june) I said sweetly, gathering up my son. Christian 'flew' the toy airplane all the way into the colorful therapy room.

As I filled out the medical questionnaire, a heavyset nurse with bright orange lipstick and three piercings on each ear greeted us cordially. She motioned to a stack of blocks. "This is to see if he can stack the blocks without being told to," she said. I wanted to point out to her that she said that right in front of Christian but didn't want to start off his first therapy session on the wrong foot. Christian looked at the blocks without any interest and then flew his toy plane over them. *Yup, this is going to go just great!*

A few minutes later, the actual occupational therapist entered the room. "Hello Christie, I'm Megan. Being that this is your first time here, I'm sure you're both a little nervous. The first thing I want to say is to not worry about anything. As we chat and get to know each other a little bit, I'm going to see what Christian does. That doesn't sound scary, does it?"

I liked Megan. After a few minutes of conversation, Christian noticed the blocks. He carefully landed his toy airplane and picked up one of the blocks and put it in his mouth as he began to stack the others.

"He's seeking sensory input," Megan informed me. I had done a lot of initial research, so I knew what that meant.

"He puts things in his mouth often but because he's so young I thought perhaps he was teething."

She proceeded to inform me of the differences between teething and requiring sensory input. I was able to ask a lot of questions which she calmly answered. However, by the time we left, I was dazed. I was walking through the tunnel of someone else's life.

Chapter 6

Life is unfair

"I find the best way to love someone is not to change them, but instead, help them reveal the greatest version of themselves."
Steve Maraboli

On the way home, I couldn't stop the tears from falling. I kept glancing at Christian in the rear-view mirror to see if he noticed, but he was flying his toy airplane over the trees outside. I wanted to scream. I wanted to sob loudly. Yet, I couldn't for Christian's sake. I didn't want him to think he made Mommy sad. So, I drove with the radio on, silently crying, unable to stop the torrent of tears running down my cheeks.

This is so unfair! What did we do to deserve this? What does this mean for us? For Christian? I was having trouble focusing on driving.

I thought of the kids I had seen in the waiting

room... *how can God do this to all those families? Is there even a God?*

I took in a deep breath, wondering if I was going to allow myself to ask the question, *God, are you real?*

I racked my brain for something, anything I had heard while attending the many Catholic Masses over the years to restore my faith in God. Yet, my faith was afraid to step up and convince me that God, in fact, was real.

When George came home from work, he chatted about a belligerent, drunken customer who wouldn't leave the liquor store. I laughed at how animated George was, particularly when he started imitating the woman who had upset him. I actually forgot for a moment that I had just taken our son to his first therapy session for autism and that I was beginning a new life that I absolutely hated.

"Hey," he said later, while we were eating dinner, "how'd it go today?"

I gave him vague details while I screamed on the inside. George has always been a caring and happy person, and as he was telling me the story of the woman at the store, I realized that I would keep much of my angst from him. I needed him happy; I needed his warmth. I didn't think I would be able to survive the desert of being a mother with an autistic child without his passion for life.

That night as I prepared to go to sleep, I took off the cross pendant necklace I wore. I didn't think anything of it as I walked away from it on the dresser. A few minutes later, when I went back to the dresser for something else, I saw it there...the cross was slanted over the uneven coil of the necklace. I wondered again if God was real and if I would ever wear that cross again.

"I don't think I need you right now," I said softly to the cross chain, "Christian is now the cross I must carry."

Chapter 7

Our New Normal

"I am beautiful, not broken. Different, not less. Challenged, not challenging. Overwhelmed, not spoiled. Autism is not a choice however, acceptance is."
Center for Autism

Before Christian was two, I took up residence in a dark place in our kingdom to protect myself from my crumbling world. Everything I had known as my life was disappearing. All hopes that nothing was wrong with Christian were dashed. Outings with Christian to church and play dates were no longer fun. His outbursts had increased in number and intensity. Activities we'd done in the past were crossed off my list of what Christian and I could do successfully. People's reactions and sometimes their attitudes were more than I could handle. However, I did continue to take Christian with me on short shopping trips when I had groceries to get, drug store errands, or an occasional appointment.

I had a favorite shopping center chain store; it was close to home and basic one-stop shopping. Like most toddlers, Christian liked riding in the shopping cart. However, all the visual stimulation irritated him. When set down on the floor he would crawl around under the display racks. One day he acted up, and I had a meltdown over the impatience and what seemed like plain rudeness of an employee. She had acted irritated because my child was misbehaving. I asked her, "Can you please move that rack so I can see those clothes?" She ignored my request and walked away from us with an annoyed look. I tried to apologize to her and explain that he is not typical, but again she ignored me.

I found a manager and told him, "My son has autism and I know he's misbehaving, but there is no need for your employee to ignore my attempts to speak with her." The manager said he would talk to the employee and walked over to her. However, he never came back to me with any sort of apology. So, I told another manager how frustrated I was and explained I shopped there once a week and was a good customer. Again, I got no apology or acknowledgment of understanding. He looked at me like I was a bad parent. It was a look I was resenting more and more. I told him "No one here is hearing what I'm saying. I don't want to shop here anymore."

My dark place grew to include that whole store.

Because my son, and most autistic children, doesn't appear to have a disability, when he misbehaves, he looks like a handsome little boy acting like a spoiled brat child with a bad mother. The looks we got in that store that day were awful looks that made for an awful day. We had many similar bad experiences. My son would have a screaming fit in a restaurant or bolt for the door. I would have to grab his hand or shirt and grip tightly. That makes him scream as if in pain, and it looks like I'm abusing him. I get horrible stares and people shaking their heads in disapproval of me.

My dark place was expanding into more and more of the world. A raw, deep hatred of people's behaviors grew inside me like a virus. In time, I reached the point where I didn't care if we bothered anyone. I would explain to those who looked concerned, but most people didn't want to hear anything I had to say.

That is when my online shopping started. It is how I do most of my shopping now. It's just easier.

Like store outings, play dates were no longer a good idea. Christian didn't interact with the other children; he had no interest in them. The moms of the typical children seemed to pity me. I didn't want anyone's pity. We don't merit pity.

Most Sundays at church I ended up outside chasing Christian around. I decided I'd rather worship at home. I can pray at home. Plus, I wasn't ready to share what our world was like; I was still grieving the dissolution of normalcy and learning my way around our new norm.

The New Diet

A huge part of my learning concerned Christian's conditions and their physical symptoms, hand in hand with his nutritional needs. Christian has symptoms caused by the same underlying issues as most autistic people: chronic inflammation, oxidative stress, gastrointestinal dysfunction, immune dysregulation. These issues are affected in his behavior, bowel, and sleep problems.

In her book The Un-Prescription for Autism, Dr. Janet Lintala, founder of the Autism Health center and an autism mom herself states, "Correcting these overlooked conditions with digestive enzymes, probiotics, antifungals, and other non-psychiatric treatments brings transformative results: less pain, less aggression, and a child who is more receptive to behavioral and educational interventions." But, I didn't know much about these conditions as Christian was due to transition from a bottle to baby food. And most of what his pediatrician recommended seemed to treat his symptoms, not the causal conditions.

So, we went through frustrating weeks of food drooling onto his chin, spoons being batted out of my hand; less in his tummy, more on the floor. I tried everything his early doctors recommended; while he did let me know what he liked and didn't, no new foods or supplements seemed to help his bowels or his behavior---my two biggest nemeses. By the time he was two, together we had come to agreement on his favorite foods and most helpful menus.

Breakfast was apples or gluten-free cereal with almond milk with probiotics and his favorite, Cocoa Loco bars by Enjoy Life. Lunch became gluten-free diary-free crullers with coconut peanut butter, a bit of oven-gold Boars Head turkey, and fruit snacks or a cookie and applesauce. After a nap, snack time could be Happy Tots, pretzels with hummus, fruit salad or a peach. Dinner choices advanced to include chicken, sweet potato, peas or lentils with peas or peas with rice, gluten-free pizza (no cheese) with beef, baked potato or pot roast. Lots of good choices. He liked all these menu items and often the whole family could dine the same...me, Dad George, and Big Sister Brianna.

By the time Christian was two, I was ready to give alternative medicine/holistic medicine a try. Dr. Springer, a homeopathic doctor, who came to me well recommended, offered us myriad options on dietary helps for Christian. He shared his position with me that autism symptoms originate in the gut--to heal the brain, you start with the gut. So first, we put Christian on a gluten-free and casein-free diet (GFCF, also known as gluten-free diary-free GFDF). Casein is a protein found in all mammals' milk. Research exists showing that people with ASD have an abnormal immune response to the protein in casein as well as the proteins in gluten (grains including wheat, oats, barley, rye).

The list of foods containing these tough to digest proteins is very long, the most common being milks, ice cream, sour cream, yogurt, butter, some lunchmeats, and cheese; the list of foods that don't contain them is much shorter. Parents will try to keep researching all updates to stay current on both lists. Using our list from Dr. Springer, within three days the improvement in Christian was apparent. He started talking more, and his bowel movements were more normal. Between 2014 and 2016, I tried many different things; I even tried camel milk, which I now know is on the no-no list. As a mom, you'll use anything, try anything, to help your child and never stop trying but also keep on researching.

Now-two years later, there are more options out there; grass-fed meats, specialized breads. I have become a label guru. "Enjoy Life" has a great line of snacks for ASD. You can find gluten-free/diary-free baked goods, even cupcakes which we all like. Pineapple juice is good for Christian, but no juice boxes. Fiji water is great for hydration and removes aluminum and its toxicities from the brain. There is a lot to research about aluminum and the brain, and you'll read varying information on the subject. I found great information in an article by Paul Fassa, *contributing staff writer for REALfarmacy.com*, entitled, "Aluminum Poisoning." Dr. Fassa explains that there has been a dramatic increase in neurological diseases linked to aluminum.

"Aluminum accrues to toxic levels over time in slow apoptotic cell turnover tissues, such as bone matter, the heart, and the brain. The brain and its associated nervous system is where diseases such as Alzheimer's, Parkinson's, MS, chronic fatigue and other neurological or auto-immune diseases manifest, including the complete autistic spectrum, from learning disorders to full blown autism."

The second part of Fassa's article features the scientific research presented by *Dr. Chris Exley in his Message to the 2011 Vaccine Safety Conference. Fassa's article explains that a central part of Dr. Exley's conference presentation... "concerned helping vaccinated kids improve their neurological damage. Ironically, it involves the second most abundant mineral in mother earth – silica. Exley has put kids who had autism spectrum disorders or other neurological damage from vaccinations on a form of silica known as silicic acid with excellent results."

Dr. Exley's research is well worth reading and discusses mineral waters that contain high levels of silicic acid. Dr. Exley explains that there are three commercial bottled waters listing silica amounts as milligrams (mg) per liter on the bottle. Fiji has the highest amount of the three. Personally, I now use Fiji water for Christian and my whole family.

Having the whole family eating the same diet as Christian can only help all of us live a healthier, better life. Christian improves daily. For his fifth birthday, this year we went to Lego Land. He loves hotels. Lego Land was fun for all of us, and Christian was so happy when he opened the present he'd asked for, a giant fire station set. We ended the day with supper at TGI Friday's like a typical happy family, enjoying a little boy's birthday. Things are looking up!

Dr. Janet Lintala, founder of the Autism Health Center and an autism mom herself, shares the natural protocols used in her practice to dramatically improve the function and well-being of children on the spectrum. Drawing on the latest research developments, as well as personal and clinical experience, she targets the underlying issues (chronic inflammation, oxidative stress, gastrointestinal dysfunction, immune dysregulation) associated with the behavior, bowel, and sleep problems so common to autism.

Correcting these overlooked conditions with Similase Junior, digestive enzymes, by Integrative Therapeutics, probiotics- VSL #3 by The Living Shield, antifungals, and other non-psychiatric treatments brings transformative results: less pain, less aggression, and a child who is more receptive to behavioral and educational interventions.

While the medical profession is slow to change, autistic kids need help immediately. *The Un-Prescription for Autism* provides clear explanations, detailed protocols, and examples to help parents act quickly to restore their child's health, self-control , and language—paving the way for reaching their full potential.

Learning During Our New Norm

My growth during that adjustment period taught me many good, strong lessons. I learned that I can never judge others; no one can judge anyone objectively because we have no idea what others may be living with or going through. No one needs a pity party put on for them.

Now, two years later, people come to me because they know I won't judge them. I am understanding our new norm more and want to share with others what I've learned.

I've also become a strong person. I confidently believe in myself and others. I see the good in everything and everyone and try to bring positivity out in myself and others.

Christian is progressing and will start kindergarten this fall at Forest Lakes Elementary, a public school with excellent goals for atypical children. They have an amazing Autism program. He will be in a classroom with teachers trained on how to educate the whole child. He will have lunch, recess, and gym with typical peer models. His intellect is clearly good, and he loves learning. We are all ready to start kindergarten.

All is well in the Kingdom of New Norm; well, pretty good, I'd say.

Chapter 8

A Father's Perspective
By George Maajoun

"Autism is not a word to be feared, it's a child to be loved." – Four Sea Star

When Christian was around one, Christie took him to a doctor to be tested; she thought something was wrong. My memory isn't all that good, and I don't remember everything she shared about Christian's test and his first-year exam. But I do remember her saying autism was a possibility. My mind quickly dismissed that; I didn't believe it. I didn't give any weight to the test results; I really didn't think anything of them. In general, I am not an alarmist. At that time, I tended to be more positive than Christie-- not to say that derogatively. It was simply too early for a diagnosis. I suggested we give it time. I wasn't thinking No! This can never happen to us! I wanted more personal verification before we came to any conclusion or requested more testing.

Now, I can tell when he's acting differently. At age five, he speaks in full sentences; then again, he'll revert to less verbal communication and more gesturing. He regresses then he gets better again. There's a pattern, a recognizable pattern.

Being a Dad

When you're a dad you want your kids to like what you like--sports, music, working out, picnics, whatever. Brianna demonstrated her likes early on; that made it easy for me to foster them. Christian, however, can seem random in what he favors. I often don't know what to encourage in him. It's difficult.

It doesn't hurt me or break my heart; it's not disappointment in what he isn't as if I wish he were something else, something more typical, because I don't. It's not fear. I'm not afraid for myself or for him. Being an ASD dad to me is being capable deep within yourself of honest acceptance of your kid. You just love him. I dwell on nothing negative. I know having an atypical child is not anything God did. Not anything we did. The same things happen to many people.

Being Philosophical

I believe that 'Where there's history, there is measurable data.' That is said of science as well. I like waiting for and working toward measurable data.

Hard work rarely manifests itself as something bad unless it's borne from bad morals and ill-intended motives. I strongly believe that I'm too positively goal-orientated for my hard work to result in negativity. I neatly store my data intake. Stored categorically, in time I feel I can reach valid, helpful conclusions.

Positivity is a big part of my philosophy of life. "Stay Positive" is a strong mantra. Where is the positive in being negative? The mindset is this: if you're negative, you're not going to make things better. Your positivity can be contagious; so can your negativity. If you think negatively, your wife may feel you've given up on your child. If you're a dad, be a dad. Step up to the plate. Don't judge your own kid. Be there to support your wife and assume your kindest approach to all your roles within the family.

Of course, there's going to be conflicts. None of us is perfect or right all the time. However, because the well-being of an autistic child is involved, a meeting of the minds must be reached as soon as possible. Your child doesn't know what's best for him or her, and you and other family members will not always agree on how to handle your child. Sometimes, like all family units, you may have to agree to disagree—for a time. Christie and I recently experienced that in two areas--food being served in the house and Christian's enrollment in kindergarten.

Coming Together on Food

While many families can eat whatever they want, we locked horns on what could be brought home. I figured if I wanted to eat fries in my house, I should be able to. However, I wasn't going to doctor's appointments or tracking food reactions. It took time, but I did learn that it wasn't good for or fair to Christian because he couldn't have fries, or fried chicken, or cheese pizza! Christie and I now try to discuss all things food. I am hopeful that we can slowly teach him that it is okay for us to have individual choice. At this moment in time, grocery shopping mostly concerns Christian's diet. The biggest disadvantage to this is the cost of a specialized diet for a family of four; the advantage is we are healthier because of it.

Coming Together on School

Christian just turned five, and it's time to make decisions about school. Recently, we went to Christian's Individual Education Plan (IEP) meeting. His team was discussing what was going to happen for his kindergarten experience. I didn't want to accept their plan for him to be in an all autism classroom. Six kids to three teachers.

Christie wasn't too open-minded in that first meeting either. We both wanted our son in a regular classroom with typical kids. We know he will pattern his behavior after theirs as high functioning as he is. The food issue worries me a bit. Is he ready to see the other kids eating different foods? We haven't had time to teach him that he needs to know other people will eat things he can't. I realized it's time to start to help him learn that, otherwise we're locking him into autism, not opening him up. He is limited in his world, but we need to help him come out and interact as best as possible.

At the second meeting, the team explained our options. We could let him go to general education, but it was likely to set him up for social setbacks and educational failures.

A second option was to leave him in Pre-K one more year to let him mature more, crossing our fingers that he'd be ready for general education in kindergarten in one year. Our final option was to check out autism programs offered in different schools within the public system. We visited several. We liked what we saw at Forest Lakes. Christie was onboard immediately. When I heard Christian would share gym, all recesses, and lunch with all the kindergarteners, I came on board as well. Our hope is he will have enough time each day to pattern many typical behaviors while learning his way.

Growing in Wisdom

I've learned much this past year, but at first, I knew so little. I had many misconceptions about autism when I first heard about it. I knew what it was, but I knew nothing about the levels such as what high-functioning means. I didn't know what the spectrum was or what all was on it, and why. I was perplexed, frustrated. Christie reminds me that during that time-period I went to church often and prayed. I remember I was at peace at home with my wonderful son, but I didn't know what to do with the public.

Once while at the steakhouse, friends joined us. Some of the parents didn't realize Christian's situation. One woman asked, "Why doesn't your son sit still?" I told her he has autism, an emotional kind of mindset. His sensory gets heightened. Christian was clanking on a plate. I explained, "It isn't loud to him; he says it's a bell from a choo-choo train. To us, it's a kid hitting a plate over, and over again. If I tell him it's a little choo-choo, he hits it softer." They didn't get it. They asked if he could, please, be quiet.

Christie and I base our expectations on what we can give to the situation and what he can give. We accept Christian fully. Consistency is key. You can best help your kids along by being consistent. I believe in using positive reinforcement to encourage growth in good behavior. At work, I reward my employees through positive acknowledgment. It is a good technique.

My faith with God is unquestioning; I don't question why certain things are happening to me. I don't question God's motives. I always think, *let's do the best we can.* Things won't always go smooth. So, I try my best. Can you imagine your future and the future of your family if you don't try your best? Going to church helps me remember that. I say my prayers. Wisdom grows in me and increases my faith.

My dad recently passed, and I grew even closer in

my faith. I saw clarity in what life is about, what my father's life was about. Reflecting on him as a father gives me perspective on my life with my kids. He lived a fulfilled life.

I tell myself now, 'Raise your kids to be great adults, not to be great kids.'

PART II

As I was writing this book, it dawned on me that my son, Christian, is young. There are many more parents with older children who have autism. They have more experience and have gone through different experiences. Since my goal is for this book to be of great value to you, I reached out to parents of autistic children of all ages and asked them to write their stories. I am extremely grateful for the ones that complied:

Angela Cochran – Steven's mom

Martha Martin – Cristian's mom

Riffat Merchant – Zafirah's mom

Kathryn Luker – Patrick's mom

Melissa Mottern – Parker's mom

To top it all off, Lisa Borges, the Executive Director of the Flutie Foundation, shared the wonderful ways that organization is helping families from all over the country.

The women that wrote chapters in this book are heroes; they're heroes to their family's and my personal heroes. I think once you read these stories, they may be yours as well.

Chapter 9

The Power of Love: A Middle-Aged Mother's Story

By Angela Cochran

"I wouldn't change you for the world, but I would change the world for you."
Unknown

From the beginning, somehow, I knew that loving my child Steven was the most important thing I could do. Following diagnosis, of course, I was concerned for his quality of life and worried about how the real world would treat him. Having been bullied as a child myself, I knew just how harmful the world could be. Because of my own experience, I was determined to become his number one advocate and protector.

To be effective, I knew I had to launch myself into researching everything that was out there and become involved with every aspect of Steven's therapy. During my early reading, which took off in about 2001, my space odyssey, there was a great deal of discussion about the world in which autism spectrum children live. Publications at that time seemed to insist that parents had to learn how to live in that world, too. For me, my odyssey fueled itself slowly forward via trial and error; I truly had too many days when I took one step forward and two steps back. Eventually, I discovered that his world joined mine when I focused on what gave him JOY. Sounds simple to do, right? It wasn't. His world, where he knew quiet, safety, and joy was encapsulated behind a shield that seemed impenetrable.

In time, I discovered that what works for us is for me to identify common things that we both like and then engage him in those activities. For Steven and me all things Disney and/or music opened the shield that encased his world. Something as fun as dancing or as simple as rearranging his VHS collection (yup, VHS dates me!) proved extremely rewarding. Spectrum children, like all children, want to know you care about them and what is important to them.

One day, in an effort to connect with him, I started lining up his cars. I wasn't mimicking him but playing alongside him. Over time, he began to stop his play and take notice of mine. Eventually, he would help me or actually join MY play by lining up a car or two for me. After playing cars alongside him on several different occasions, he started including me in his play as if I totally belonged there. That was the beginning of my son seeing me. Only after I illustrated for him that his joy was my joy and that I only wanted to be near him, not change him, did I become a safe person to him. A milestone!

Spectrum people will connect with you if you are safe to connect to. If you're pushy, judgmental, and want them to be something they are not, you are not a safe person. Your child is not supposed to be like anyone else. He/she is supposed to be him/herself. Love these children for who they are, not for who you would have preferred them to be. We have an incredibly special and unique gift in these children, and they open our eyes to the world and show us how to love unconditionally. They will be your greatest blessing if you let them be. However, that does take time to learn.

My Learning Process

When Steven was a baby, his head seemed abnormally large compared to my daughters. This made me start paying attention to other red flags like the way he was never startled by anything because he appeared to be deep in thought. And, he would laugh at seemingly nothing at all. He knew and used several words by his first birthday but promptly stopped speaking after his first-year checkup. At that same time, he also began suffering from nonstop intestinal issues. Coincidently, he had received his 12-month shots at that checkup.

After researching his new symptoms, at 13 months, I asked his doctors to test him for autism. They informed me that local affiliation with Kaiser University's autism program, at that time (2000), didn't consider autism diagnostic testing until the child was at least two years old. So, I made an appointment for his second birthday. By the time that appointment time arrived, his autism was obvious and diagnosed. That catches you up to 2001, My Space Odyssey. (I even have a great theme song for that!)

Now, to catch you up on the rest of the family. My husband and other family members did not take the diagnosis well. I think my already unsteady marriage was rocked hard by the diagnosis. My marriage, for me, became more about parenting Steven than about us. The entirety of parenting a child with autism and all its implications may have been partly to blame for our divorce. Conversely, in time, my mother embraced Steven fully, and she remained loving to him until her passing. However, my father has never bonded emotionally with my son. At this point in time in my life, I know having an autistic child is wonderful. He's smart and sweet and loving. My family still thinks, after these 18 years, that Stephen is a lot of work, but I don't think so.

Steven is now fully functional. He can complete his day from start to finish on his own with only very mild prompts or reminders. On a personal note, my most recent victory with my son has been to just let him grow up. Even though I struggle with that now and then, I know the most loving thing is to let go and let him fly. I must admit I feel the discomfort of the tug of letting go right now, because, for the past six months, he has been staying with his father. This is challenging for me to accept. However, like all empty-nesters, I must find my own path and set new goals that are just for me.

I don't have any goals for Steven now other than to be available to help him achieve whatever his goals are. But, I have a few for you, the readers of this amazing book.

So, here is my Dear Angela advice: (you know the old adage "with age comes wisdom"? Well, it doesn't just come; it is hard fought and hard won, so please listen up!)

> 1. To married couples: Become a team. Don't allow any diagnosis to drive a wedge between you. The VERY BEST thing you can do for yourselves and your child is to have a healthy marriage that can support your child's growth and foster your family's future.
> 2. To single parents: Get a support system in place and make sure you take very good care of yourself. You can't save anyone if you're drowning.
> 3. To families with typical children siblings: Make sure you are supporting and loving your other children as individuals. And, do not parentize them into helping too much with their siblings. Let them be kids, not little grown-ups.

4. To all who know a spectrum person - and that is now ALL of us: Do your research, so you know everyone's limits, including your child's, your own and all those offering help. Talk to others but don't hyper focus on any diagnosis. Focus on what brings solutions for your child. Eliminate the word sick from your working vocabulary, being different is not an illness.

5. To those who first hear the diagnosis: Make factual flashcards for yourself on the points to follow and read them daily! Your child is perfect. Like all children, you will need to teach them to navigate the world and stay safe. You do not need to make your child into a replica of everyone else. Help your child become the best he/she can be. Help them thrive as they truly are. Don't try to change what makes them themselves. Accept them, guide them, uplift them, love them, realize the true meaning of love and cherish it.

6. My final advice to all families everywhere: Love your child; nothing matters more!

A Note From Christie:

First and foremost, let me get this out of the way, I love Angela. Ever since I met her, she has been an inspiration to me, not only for the way she parents her child but for her overall outlook on life. In all seriousness, she **inspires me** not only to be a better mother but teaches me that I **can be** a better mother.

I "met" Angela online and instantly felt connected to her. I actively follow her on Instagram and other social media platforms. She takes time out of her busy days to give me advice, and I'll forever be grateful to her.

I agree 100 percent with the advice she gives here:

Married couples need to become a team. Without cooperation, patience, and understanding, your child's growth will suffer.

Single parents, you need to take care of yourself first – eat well, sleep well, think positively, take up a hobby. I know you want to be selfless, but as Angela put it, you can't save anyone if you're drowning.

To families with typical children, make sure each of your children gets the love, time and affection they need. Some need more than others. Let them be kids. Sure, have them help, but don't force it.

To all who know a child with autism, educate yourself, information on autism is everywhere. Be kind, compassionate, and considerate to families that struggle in a way you don't. They didn't do anything wrong; it's not a curse. Help them, don't hurt them by your ignorance or by turning a blind eye.

Lastly to those who hear the diagnosis, this entire book is really for you. Don't panic, don't despair, it's not a death sentence. Your autistic child will give you more moments of joy than you expect.

Finally, to echo the essence of Angela's message, love one another.

Chapter 10

Faith Triumphs the Dark Ages
By Martha Martin

"Faith isn't the ability to believe long and far into the misty future. It's simply taking God at his word, and taking the next step." – Joni Erickson Tada

I dreamed of your tiny face so clear

I prayed God help me keep you near

But to the world one day you'll go

To your best dream, I know you'll want to soar

For now, I'll sing for you to hear

I sense a thrill as your time draws near

Now hush my baby, it's time to rest

Here in my womb, your sleep is best

I'm intentionally setting you up, preparing the stage for what you perhaps already know will be a plot twist. So, allow me to continue... YES, my pregnancy was typical, my preparations as a mom-to-be, from my few lines above, somewhat emotional and precious. The lines above are all I remembered. I tend to journal and love to write privately. But I could not locate what I wrote over 19 years ago.

Yes, it was the height of emotions; the time of expectations. The bond that occurs with a little someone you've never met but love as your own who happens to have a residence inside your own body. With those emotions are also moments of fright, as mom-to-be begins to realize you are part of a secret timeline, a progression of undefined seasons to come. For now, the weirdest progression is how your body takes a form of its own, an internal organ shifts as it prepares for what is the forming of new life. It was a bit "close encounter" like.

Again, remember, I am setting you up, so humor me with my next paragraph.

I have to believe every mom-to-be revisits her own timeline, her life from her own childhood, to now expecting a child of her own. To my surprise, my moments were very thought provoking and surprisingly emotional. It went something like this - As a child you play, you discover, letting imagination grow, creativity clues you into a world of make-believe; developmental strides turn out all good.

As an adolescent, all those skills go wild, sort of like controlled chaos even with the strictest parents. OK STOP! I never went further than that. My baby was still in my womb. That was enough of a progression.

Well, November 1998, Baby Cristian came into the world at 38 weeks. Hmmm! 10 Fingers, 10 toes. His dad followed him everywhere at Brigham & Women. No one was going to switch his kid.

However, it was a very hard labor, and my perfect baby had a very pointed head due to five hours of labor. BUT the baby we long waited for and planned was here wearing a little pointy hat.

Developmental Ages

I stayed with Cristian for the first 3 months and returned to work. As a product manager, I still did some traveling. Cristian had the most amazing Nanny who called me often and helped me not miss the first moments in his life. I was able to go home for lunch to be the one to first feed him solids, give him his first milk bottle and the last stash of breast milk I was able to store. She helped me be present, and I was enjoying every moment. We celebrated two birthdays that were very typical (notice I won't use the word normal).

It was my nanny that noticed that there was something wrong with Cristian. I had started a little snow globe collection of my travels, and she would hold them for Cristian. She noticed that he was too fascinated with them, and had his first tantrum when she tried to engage him. I then removed them, and he became fixated on the ceiling fan. It was at that point I knew Cristian was changing. We noticed regression in our baby especially in areas of his cognitive development that now triggered negative behaviors. Although still compliant, Cristian slowly stopped answering to his name. His use of language became less and less. He cried more, and tantrums became his new form of expression.

Cristian no longer played; he just lined things up in an order that only made sense to him. I noticed the walking on his tiptoes. I became alarmed and took him quite often to the doctor. The pediatrician did not give us answers but rather asked us to wait and give it time. OH! If I could get some of that time back. The other "experts" were able to document his delay and regression, but the prognosis was always pretty much non-conclusive. Another whole year would pass before he could be seen for a formal neurological diagnosis. By then he was almost four. In the midst of these years. I had two other boys. They are the greatest brothers for him. Life was still going on while I was finding answers for Cristian.

The Dark Ages

After tons of paperwork, recounting behaviors, reviewing the timelines of when we saw his behavior shift and regress, oh, it was not only painstaking, but time was going by, and we could not help our son. I went back to the girl in the beginning of this chapter - singing to her womb. I was confused with what was going on around me. What happened to the progression of life? We had checked off some developmental gains. We had seen him begin his progression of life. Where did my son go? We finally bereaved the son we knew. Nothing could ever compare to the pain of losing your child, the one you saw experience great moments. The body was still alive, but the soul was gone. He was not the child who sang happy birthday to himself, the one that could sing and count in both languages; the one who would giggle at the thought of being held so high with arms extended way, way, up then setting him down on top of the mantle of our fireplace as his throne for everyone to see. He could no longer stand to have his feet off the ground without it being followed by a crazed cry. As I write this I am surprised by the unexpected inability to breathe; tears are just flowing.

    The neurologist finally gave us his diagnosis PDD/NOS which meant Pervasive Development Delay / Not Otherwise Specified. The diagnosis seemed so anticlimactic given all the tests administered. So, living in Boston, the Medical Mecca of the country, their immediate prognosis was mostly clinical, which meant our little guy would be given mostly medication and psychological therapy. Access to treatment for behavioral disorder was all but non-existent. We were living through the Dark Ages of this awful disease now known as AUTISM! No one knew enough, and not much was available for our son.

We had few explanations for family and friends. Everyone around us didn't know what to say, and it felt very isolating. We were deemed pariah's, for even we had little control of our precious boy.

Discoveries in the midst

What everyone at the time failed to understand is that my son was not crazy, retarded, or handicapped. As a mom, I fought so hard to get services, schooling, to learn about him, see what made him happy, how to comfort him. I became his primary advocate. Cristian was my first-born; he was my son. He was all I knew, and I did all I could for him. We became a one income family, sold our home, sold my car, and eventually moved to Central Florida where there were more services available, and schools were already beginning to respond to those needs. Because that's what love does; it goes to the end of the earth if necessary.

As I learned more about Autism, I realized Cristian, and kids like him, are heroes. They battle to press through a myriad of sensory challenges just to try to acknowledge us. The hurdles they jump in order to do life with us is a huge victory. Let me put this in perspective. If a cement truck drives by, for most of us, it's a mere background noise. For our guys, it's not only something they hear so piercingly in their ears, but they also feel the movement inside them and are overcome by anxiety. An ordinary fluorescent light, to the natural eye, seems to be steady, but to our kiddos, they could see the actual flickering, the on and off motion that keeps itself from overheating. It explains why our kids will resort to an escape within themselves. They will play a video in their mind or sing songs or self-talk as a form of self-soothing to keep themselves stable in an overly stimulated world.

In fact, if you receive a "hello" from a child or person with Autism, please know that an onslaught of lights, noises, movements, and smells had to be quelled just so he/she can hear you enough to respond back with a "Hello."

It's like pressing through a personal war zone, thus the reason I call them heroes. But all they want is to be accepted – they have proven themselves by fighting through enormous distractions. The more breakthroughs, the easier it becomes for them. This is referred to as desensitizing.

For this reason, early intervention is so paramount. They learn to adapt and learn how to press through these changes, and WE can get better at listening to them and learn to accept them as they are. These kids work so hard to be part of our world. I wish we would press through the socially acceptable stigma and engage them in their world. How I would love to flap my arms when I'm excited or rock in my seat when I feel disoriented. I guess the nervousness can only be displayed by tapping your fingers on the desk or biting your fingernails or jiggling keys or any other "acceptable" behavior. SO, we teach our kids to learn at an early age to react in socially acceptable ways. Children with Autism also learn to change their reactions to these distractions. They can learn the socially appropriate behaviors. (I hope you notice my discontent). Our kids have enough challenges trying to fit into a world that makes it so complicated for them. Despite this, some of our kiddos may learn to adapt and engage in life with us. As a Special Needs teacher, I've taught many children behavior modifications to reduce their anxieties, but I prefer to focus on how they can press through changes in their environment.

The Crossroad

The reality of a parent in despair and hopelessness is a continual fight. The no cures, the devastation of life as you knew it. You are consumed by the inability to do life like other friends and families. Being escorted out of public places (restaurant, movies, supermarkets, play dates) because they do not understand your journey. How about not being invited to gatherings, parties, picnics, because they fear you may actually attend. It's an isolating feeling. You end up pushing away the very people that care because you are afraid they too will reject you. So, despair strikes; there is no cure, and no one accepts you. Some stories end with parents committing suicide, or the child found dead in dumpsters. It's a reminder that the struggles we face generally take us to this crossroad. It's in those crossroads that we make decisions of life. Some face these crossroads daily. No one is exempt. I believe at some point, we all can somewhat relate to the depth of pain that drove the parent to make such a horrific decision. Just being transparent right now. Even the most God-believing people have those moments when they doubt they can hold on. The question they ask themselves is, how much is too much?

There is no simple answer. Most of the time the choice is to redirect our thoughts. This is not over simplifying the grief, but to share what has helped me in the dyer moments that I faced, not just with my son, but in life's adversities. In the scriptures, Paul talks about doing our best by filling our minds and meditation on things that are true, noble, reputable, authentic, compelling and gracious, the best not the worst; the beautiful not the ugly; things to praise not things to curse. Do that and God, who makes everything work together, will work you into his most excellent harmonies (Phil 4:6-8).

It was faith in the WORD that somehow rose up through deep despair.

The Loss

I spoke about of the obvious loss; the one of your dearest child as you knew them. Another big loss that is slowly, quietly, losing life, in this new undefined progression, is the marriage. For families with a child with autism, there is no blueprint on how to do life. The spectrum is vast, the depth of the condition can only be defined by the family. For anyone to compare their situation to another's is so unfair, because there is no way to gauge the urgency for the family being affected. If you feel blessed because you see another family who has it worse, well, there is more than just autism affecting your family. Time to do a self-check. You see, the urgency is real and not to be compared. Each family affected has to spend dedicated time to discover the details of their child; the diagnosis, the plan of attack, the impact on the family, how their lives will change. Autism may not be the single factor. There may be other ailments going on. The family as a whole is affected, and to juggle life, it will take a strong marriage to keep it together. The essence of doing life in a marriage can be lost in the shuffle. Many couples begin to live parallel lives. Especially, when the mother is the most involved, the nurturing aspect seems to be minimal due to the juggling and exhaustion.

Some couples cannot survive the grieving process. Remember the mom-to-be at the beginning of this chapter? In a similar way, Dads also had dreams for the child they awaited. These were also crushed by the newfound need. Some can, with help, be more accepting of their new reality and begin to draw new dreams. However, most couples begin to realize there is a separation that is not only physical but emotional. Many times, it takes years before the realization that parallel lives have occurred. I believe the percentage of divorce in a Special Needs family is staggering. The last statistic I recall was in the 80th percentile.

This is not what the couples planned. Life throws curve balls. Life is unpredictable. Autism was not part of that progression.

Life with a child/adult with autism is very challenging, and living is at a high emotional cost. Not everyone will want to continue; some spouses may decide this is not what they thought life would be. Although I cannot attribute my divorce entirely on my son's autism, I do believe the distance, and parallel living eventually may have caused a strain. Personally, it was my faith that caused me to move on during these unexpected losses. As a single mother, I am grateful for the strength and fortitude, and for the extra dose of love to be the sole nurturing parent for my boys. As the main source of influence, I am transparent with them and always teach life lessons by modeling them, especially when I ask them for forgiveness.

The Gains

Autism impacted how we do life as a family. For many years, we were unable to go away on vacations or change our routines. A mere change of temporary residence would be at a great cost to our lives. HOWEVER, with a lot of work, patience, and perseverance, we now enjoy taking trips. In fact, Cristian is able to take a plane ride! In 2015, we spent 15 days in NYC. Change was everywhere, noise was everywhere, and not to mention the people. CHRISTMAS IN NEW YORK was the best way to showcase how far Cristian has come. A huge part of this I can wholly attribute to our faith and all the prayers and support. For it's our faith that allowed us to see beyond what was in front of us. It was HIS Grace that elevated us to see beyond our present situation.

I wanted to take this time to also showcase the amazing brothers Cristian has and how they have blessed my life. Daniel and Adam are the best siblings I could ever ask for Cristian. GOD has instilled in them a heart of compassion like no other. They are kids that have learned to live without, and yet be content with what is. Sure, they have been able to participate in a typical life environment, but there have been interruptions that have paralyzed us as a family, not just Cristian's journey, but with me as a single mom. They have stepped up to support me and have become my encouragers. I have also re-engaged with my family. I feel their love and support more than ever. Like I mentioned, sometimes we isolate ourselves, and we forget that there are those who love us and want to help. I travel often to see them, and they get to enjoy Cristian and we have a beautiful bond. Cristian loves to go see his Tía's and Tío's, his cousins and his 95-year-old Abuela.

The Triumphs

The mere fact that Cristian regained significant verbal ability is monumental. Because of the extensive ABA therapy, and the Speech, OT, and PT that were available, we were able to work with him at home along with the schools (both public and private) and his therapists. I sometimes think of the years lost waiting for a diagnosis. But I quickly move on. Every day is a gift. Every acknowledgment, every unprompted social involvement, every spontaneous word, every I LOVE YOU, MOM (which gets me each time) is a huge milestone. We count it all joy!! We have learned not to take any emotion, any word, or any reaction for granted. It's all huge!

Cristian will remain with me in his safe home as he is transitioning into adulthood and beyond. He is now quite independent and can care for himself. He is capable of learning a trade and growing in the ability to use some skills. Despite the inability to receive the extent of early intervention, I feel that GOD has brought him way up to speed because of HIS love. With that, I still continue to dream for Cristian. I still envision greater things for him. I am amazed at how much he has overcome to be the man he is. He is an amazing piano player and has the most amazing voice. My DEEPEST appreciation to all the teachers, therapists (Speech, OT, PT Behavioral), the paraprofessionals, his music teacher, Cristian's doctors, and all my friends and families that have pushed down that door to be part of this journey. I am grateful to those that were persistent and became part of our lives even when I tried to push them out.

I hold on to my faith and know a miracle is possible. The hardest challenges are behind us. Now, I get to enjoy life a lot more with my boy; with all my boys. My greatest miracle is that each day, without fail, I have new joy to do it again. I am grateful each day for the blessings. I am grateful for my progression of life!! I believe we have experienced a higher level of living and loving, walking along with Cristian in his journey.

Let's see what tomorrow brings!

A word to parents dealing with a recent diagnosis.

If you are new to the autism world, do not fear the label! It's a bit of a nebulous name, but it will open doors for services. Some kiddos respond quickly, and some like mine, will take years, but they DO respond! What is in front of you is not your be all and end all. Continue to have hope. The vision for your child may be a bit different than prior to the diagnosis, but plenty of room for greatness awaits your family. Do seek counseling as a family, creating a safe place for each member to share and grow. Do not be afraid to ask your extended family, church community or friends for support. Having meals offered to you, and babysitting services so you can get away, will be your strength, and allow others to stay well versed on what your child needs. Many people will come into your child's life, but no one loves him like you do. No one is as invested as you are. You know your child, and will make the right decisions. YOU ARE ALWAYS THE EXPERTS!!! Never doubt your abilities nor your love for your child.

A Note From Christie:

Faith, hope, and joy are blessings. Miracles are not always apparent, but they happen. Your child will make you stronger and help you see the world from a different perspective. You may question your faith and beliefs at some point, but once you realize your child is a blessing, it'll be eye opening. Every little win will be an unexpected miracle.

Put good intentions out into the world and focus on what you believe in; focus on the positive, what you want for your child. Let go of the negative, and you'll be surprised at the results. Miracles, even small ones, are still miracles.

Chapter 11

One World
By Riffat Merchant

Autism is represented by a puzzle piece... not because we are puzzling; not because we are supposed to be made to fit; not because we want to be saved; but rather, because Autism is a PIECE of who we are, a PIECE of the whole of who we are.

Our beautiful five-year-old daughter is Zafirah, which means victorious. In the past three years, she and our family have been victorious already over some of the hurdles of Zafi's Autism. Being a speech pathologist, special education teacher, and an Autism Mom, I change hats several times a day. In practice, that doesn't always help Zafi, and it gives me lots of bad hair days! Seriously, I think my background makes me my own best friend and my own worst enemy. And often keeps me up at night!

From the beginning, I switched at will, and often from habit, from teacher mode to mommy mode. Throughout Zafi's entire first year I loved playing with her. At times, she enjoyed playing alone, which I was thankful for; it gave me time to do my chores. She particularly loved her first puzzles and would do them over, and over again while I spruced up room after room. My husband and I adored her docile personality and the fact that she waited in her bed upon waking and didn't cry or call for us.

Around the time of her first birthday, I decided to start tracking her development. She wasn't making animal sounds, you know, baa for sheep, moo, meow, and she hadn't spoken any words, not even dada or mama. I knew something wasn't quite right, but I assumed the "let's wait and see" perspective. When she was 21 months old I became pregnant (a planned pregnancy) and it was then that I decided Zafi needed a full work up. I wanted to get all her testing completed before delivery of her baby brother and to start her in speech therapy as well, even though I am ADHD with co-morbid visual perception/processing (eye/ear to brain cross-wiring) and knew a great deal about that condition. Zafi seemed completely opposite of me. Although the diagnosis was another three months away, enough results trickled in that we knew she was definitely somewhere on the Autism Spectrum. I sprang into action. I enrolled her in a language class at a nearby YMCA, and I realized I needed to go back on my meds in order to bring out the best in Zafirah. I needed focus.

By her second birthday we had her "autistic" diagnosis and learned that she lived in her own world, a world we had to learn to enter. We had no idea how to do that, but we learned. Zafi's world has immensely changed over the past three years since she was two. At first, it was all about me joining her play. I got down on the floor with bubbles and blew my face red. I colored, finger painted, squished play dough. Although my mommy hat sat firmly on my head, I must admit, I also used my teaching strategies from the past to work play with Zafi. I was constantly analyzing her strengths to use them to increase her weaknesses. Her greatest weakness was communication. I decided to be her communication guru, her Mama Yoda.

She was learning best when I combined showing her with telling her words. I made flash cards (and laminated them!) for everything I could. One day, I even took her to the mall to ride the escalator repeatedly, just to teach her the words up and down. She mastered it and Mama Yoda was venturing away from home with her in tow.

Next, I taught her gardening and how to water plants. She toted about her little, bright-yellow, sprinkling can and matching little, plastic spade. I tried my wings at film-making, creating videos of what we'd done... complete with voice over. I would plop her down on the couch, and she would watch the videos and listen to my recording as many times as I'd hit replay. That helped her so much!! And I, of course, cleaned.

At about that same time, I learned that to help her best I needed to plan every minute of her day. Or, maybe I needed to plan every minute of MY day with her. Far and away, her favorite, joyful activity was bubbles, so I printed "Play Bubbles" into her daily schedule. To this day she loves bubbles and now plays them with her little brother. Over and over I had to teach her normal things like coloring and talk her through it, which was a technique I'd learned at the university when I was studying speech pathology. Puzzles became her next love. I hate puzzles! I'm not good at them. Well, Zafi loves puzzles and they calm her. So, sigh, I entered her world of puzzles.

Each, and every day I anticipate her world, plan her schedule, and observe when other people work with her. After her second birthday, the time arrived for me to take her out into social settings, into society, which is a very gray world with streams and swirls of overlapping, intertwined skills.

There is no overlapping gray in Zafi's world. Her world is black and white!

It is up to me to plan for and prep her each time she must enter our gray world. For example, I discovered my sister-in-law is a puzzle whiz, so play dates with Aunt Zolfa were penned into the schedule. Birthday parties entered Zafi's world, and I learned how to walk and talk her through musical chairs and balloons. We practiced at home for days before a party. She had started talking and was making progress. We continued filling her days with classes, therapies, play dates, oh so many play dates.

She had music and marching classes, her little feet shuffling along. Oh, and Gymboree. Anything and everything to immerse her with other kids. Birthday parties forever loomed as the most difficult because the birthday song would literally make her flip out. However, regardless of how hard it was to predict what all would be going on at a party, although I always prepped her for each event she struggled with the darn birthday song.

    One unfortunate day, when she was two and a half, she spotted the bright, neon colored flowers on a tea cozy sitting on my father-in-law's kitchen counter. Attracted by the flowers and texture of the cozy, she reached up, grabbed hold and pulled it off. I heard the screams, the crash of the kettle. She received major burns on her hips. She quit talking after that, and she seemed to have a Post-Traumatic Stress Disorder (PTSD) type reaction to kids touching her on the playground at Montessori School. I seemed to be having a PTSD aversion to taking her back out into the gray world. Her Montessori teacher reached out to me one day. "Perhaps, dear, the burns helped her in the long run because her speech didn't just return, it is blossoming." A window had opened with her speech, so I acted on it, working triple time on her communication skills. Yeah, I know. That was Teacher Hat.

    However, I still had to force myself to take her out in public. She had become a very picky eater too. I struggled to learn what she could or would eat and why. Restaurants were off the table. Instead, I became Kitchen Mom, the Dietician. I read everything written on Mind/Body/Gut (MBG), and why Autistic kids can't process gluten and/or dairy products, why they hold their bladder or bowel. I spoke to my husband about my trial and error efforts of Zafi's right diet and insisted he wasn't listening or that he just didn't get how frustrating it was... and what I was actually doing! Being a Type A, ENT doctor, his response was quick and complete. "I understand what you are doing. Autism is like a Black Box. It is a Black Box, and one by one you are checking off all the body systems inside that box." Sometimes he can be so irritatingly correct! However, I know that because he has the ability to analyze and then share and I share then analyze, we make a great team. He is also the one who predicted that our son, Zeeshan, "will be the normalizing factor in our family." And, indeed, he is. Zee loves his big sister and seems to have little trouble walking in a world that is black, white, and gray.

Regarding Zee's arrival, Marta Blanford from Early Steps, an early intervention therapy, federally funded for kids with disabilities up to age 5, cautioned us, "When your son is born, be sure he is around normal kids so he doesn't mimic Zafi or withdraw." And so, just as his father predicted, Zee's need to be around 'normal' got us all back out into the fifty shades of normal gray.

Now that they are six and four, Zafi and Zee enjoy playing together and even quarrel like all siblings. I'm likely to hear "Don't touch that!" or "Get out of my room!" from either one of them. They also share friends, play dates sometimes, and parties. Most of the time, they both behave normally, well, as normal as any kid is normal. Recently, however, when they invited their friends to visit the new house we had moved to, the friends were so excited and racing around to explore room after room shouting, "Look at this!" my two took refuge on the living room couch, huddled together in amazement at their frenzy.

Last month I took Zafi to a movie. I sat next to her thinking *we're just sitting here, watching a movie. It's so normal!* Zafi had gone with her class the week before to see, "Moana," so "Trolls" was her second movie theater outing. We brought along her friend Inaara.

Zafi knows this year that she has friends and treasures them.

She has very strong facial recognition skills now and knows when a friend has stopped coming around, whether it's one of her friends or one of ours. We have lost a few. I call them "Fleeting Friends" and accept that this happens. What's more important to share is how Zafi reached this facial recognition/awareness pinnacle. I started her "I know that face" campaign using relatives she saw frequently. I kept all their photos out, and we would name them each day; I added it to her daily schedule. Eventually, I had people send me photos of their houses, their pets, even their living rooms so that we could prep for upcoming visits. Now I use the Internet to find pictures of anything or any place I need.

"Use Visuals" was Cardinal Rule #1 that I used my first-year teaching, a year which I now refer to as my "Baptism through Hell." I had Autistic students, more challengingly, I had their Warrior Parents. These precious children looked normal, and many parents insisted on "all things normal" even though that wasn't a normal teaching/learning technique for their kids. My mentor at college had used the term Warrior Parent saying they have an overpowering angst about their child that is so strong it earns the parent a spot on the spectrum. I knew clearly what she meant... then. Later, I had to force myself to remember that when I became one of those parents. My professor had also said, "Don't become a band wagon teacher jumping onto every trend or into every fad that the parents or others bring up to you. Don't use the trendy and unproven; focus on Functional Evidence-Based Teaching Strategies." When I entered the tumbling world of ABA, Gluten Free, Casein Free, Vaccinate Don't Vaccinate, MGB, public school, private school, I reminded myself I don't have to jump on any band wagons. Because every child is unique, not one of those things is totally right or totally wrong 100% of the time for any or all of our children.

I made a decision years ago to be Zafi's communication warrior as well as a plain and simple good parent. Right now, her speech is being refined. She's in a private, non-denominational school because she seems to need a small group and rigorous environment. We had her in private, then two preschool years in public, and now back in private. Once we started private, this most recent time and she thrived, we decided to stay private the whole way.

And she's thriving at home, too. She announced this spring, "I want a new bike." I replied, "First you learn to ride your old bike without its training wheels." So, off came the wheels. She fell and fell and ran away, came back and fell some more. When she is challenged, she must work through it. She needs for me to just step back. Also, we have added Nani Night School to Zafi's routine. My mother, Nani, started teaching Zafi handwriting on an iPad two years ago. Zafi enjoys time with Nani as a break from her dad and me. Also, we now accept and occasionally solicit help from others.

And many others help us indeed. It takes a village.

A Note From Christie:

> I know Rif personally, she was a volunteer at Cypress Woods Elementary School when Christian was three. We'd received his diagnosis and had gone through training at Early Steps. She would work with Christian. When there was a party, I would go, and that's how I met her. She would tell me how wonderful he was. Due to our schedules and busy lives, we don't often get together, but when it happens we catch up.
>
> She talks about Floor play, and visual learning. They are very important. What she learned from Marta, from early steps, I learned as well. Every child is unique in their own way, whether

they're in whatever spectrum. My question becomes this; what's normal anyway?
"I adore him. I love him"
I'm happy for Christian that he got to spend time with such an amazing and loving person.

Chapter 12

Early Detection

By Katheryn Luker

> *"Autism causes stress, anxiety, depression, isolation, money, marital & family problems. Austism is a constant worry & is the unknown.*
>
> *What can be done to change this?*
>
> *Be strong, stay positive, stick together, support each other, love each other & fight for what we believe in... Our children."* - unknown

Immediately after our bubbly, brown-eyed baby Patrick had his MMR Vaccinations, I saw big, disturbing changes in him. Suddenly, he started eating dirt, strings, and cloth. He quit making eye contact, quit using age appropriate speech, and started flapping (clenching and unclenching) his hands. He stopped smiling; his smile was just gone and nothing made him smile. He had smiled broadly throughout his whole first year. It was easy to see that my once gregarious baby had quit being social. He had lost his happy personality and I couldn't find it anywhere. I realized I needed to work at reversing whatever had happened to him. And I had to do it fast.

That drastic change crashed in on him one March day in 1999. By June I had him receiving services. I started a rigorous ABA Program by 2000. I wasn't surprised when we found out that something was definitively wrong because the change we'd witnessed was so shockingly obvious. I didn't get thrown into self-pity or go through a denial stage over his autism diagnosis as severe, because I just knew I didn't have any time to waste. I had no time to sit around on my pity pot; I had to run full steam ahead. I became a mother on a mission to help my son. I'm a very proactive person and needed to be proactive on his behalf. He qualified for Sooner Start on June 6. Before the new millennium rolled in, I had him in a rigorous ABA Program.

Face the Early Years with Fire in Your Belly

I cannot emphasize enough how urgently your child needs your early dedication. You have much to learn and do! You need to research the Autoimmune System. You need to learn that recovery is real if you start helping when your child is very young. Nobody else will fight this fight for your child like you. Don't accept what well-intentioned people in the medical and education systems tell you by their word alone; ask for documentation. It is essential from the beginning of your mission that you do behavioral things in the home and do them 24/7. It's hard and exhausting, but your hard work will pay off.

Here are more pieces of functional wisdom I am compelled to share with young parents. Tighten your seat belts; this is a roller coaster ride. Here we go! Don't waste any time grieving or in the denial stage. You don't have time for any of that! Request the Cunningham Panel to see whether your child has PANDAS and/or PANS *(look these up, write them down, and learn them)*. Use chelation to remove toxins from your child's body. Start giving your child probiotics. Quit vaccinating your child until big pharma quits poisoning our kids with preservatives in the vaccines! Study autoimmune disorders. Feed your mind and soul by reading. Read my book "If He Were Your Son." Read "I Know You're in There," by Marcia Hinds. Study and stay current with an Applied Behavioral Analysis (ABA) Program, and **read and use this book** for guidance and inspiration.

This advice is based on my truths. Your truths are what you will determine they are; once determined, they will dictate your battle plan. You have to get yourself to a strong, educated, definitive place. There are plenty of opinions in the analysis of autism. You'll need to nurture and/or change your opinions, and I dare say you'll change them more than once, into your steadfast truths and stick to them.

Establish Your Support and Start at Home

Nineteen years ago, we were a young family working and living in McAlester, Oklahoma. Following Patrick's diagnosis at his first birthday, my husband and I charted our course of action. Because he was already very busy at work and I had already dived right into the autism river, we declared that my husband would be the architect and maintenance engineer of our ship; I would be captain. I'd enlist whatever crew we agreed was good for our son, and I'd sail our ship right into the future, and none of us would ever look back. I knew I could keep us on course, regardless of high, frothing waves, raging storms, and frightening lightening and that I would never lose sight of safe ports in the storm, points of respite or our destination.

All too often, school blew our ship about like a bobber. Each time my hands clenched the wheel tighter, refusing to loosen. I learned to go to every school meeting fueled up and running full steam ahead. Like a good captain, I logged all my always very specific objectives each step of the way throughout Patrick's school years, noting his educational, social, and emotional experiences, both his progressions and his regressions.

I worked with the school system to ensure that his ABA program was followed, at least on SOME points. I had to ardently insist that the school hire an aide to be with him at all times. I fought to make the district give him services during the summer months.

I published a book detailing our trials and triumphs living with autism and that helped clarify for me and others why help for the whole child needs to be offered by the school, not just the parents. In general, however, cooperation from the public-school system was a fight from day one. Yes, I won some battles on behalf of Patrick, but there were too many battles I never should have had to fight. Patrick has had many good teachers and other staff support, but, overall, all staff members work for the school district and the principles of the school system, and they must comply or risk losing their jobs. In most parts of the country, those who assist with state or federal programs have even more limiting guidelines that they must follow, and those programs are shared among many districts. This can result in infrequent visits to any one school district and the slighting of a child's needs.

Own Your Present

Today, as Patrick transitions into the adult world, he has achieved many victories and still faces many challenges. My son has conquered his behavioral issues. He talks and can easily say what he wants or doesn't want as far as food, activities, and loads of other likes and dislikes. He takes care of his own hygiene, shaves himself, cooks microwave meals, ties his tennies and belts his jeans (unlike average teens), loves swimming, and has so many more skills. He still faces challenges. He cannot express himself in a spontaneous manner, have abstract ideas or conversations, or meaningful two-way conversations.

He isn't driving, experiencing deep friendships, or close personal relationships. These are things he may one day choose to set as goals for himself.

Currently, however, Oh Captain My Captain is his closest friend. Patrick enjoys being with me, and I enjoy his friendship and company. In fact, Patrick is one of my best friends, and I'm the one person he has available to do things with him. We grew up together that way. I had almost no friendships while raising him because I was completely busy with his ABA program at home. However, since he now controls his social behaviors, my parents and select other people take him to do things like go to the movies, out to eat, and to church events. These are good times for him.

Know Where You Stand

The goals I mentioned above that Patrick may one day strive for probably don't seem realistic to many of you, but when you believe in recovery, then these goals are realistic. Since I started addressing my son's medical diagnosis of PANS so late in his life, I don't know about the likelihood of a full recovery for him. That is why it's VERY important that parents of young autistic children address their medical issues right away, including testing for physical infections caused by strep, or possibly by Lime's Disease, Mono, or other diseases that compromise the immune system. These are treatable and curable, but not if you never have them tested for diagnosis. If diagnosed, follow through with medical treatment.

While opinions fly wide and freely and clinical trials continue to grow world-wide, two very clear and opposing stances continue to grow about the best path of diagnosis and treatment for autism. We could call this "the great divide," and it has become as divisive as the Mason-Dixon Line. One group of people, the larger group, thinks that autism is okay and that we should accept it as an it-is-what-it-is condition. People in this group also believe that we should accept the child's diagnosis and learn to adapt to their world. The majority of the autism organizations focus on acceptance of the autistic person's world and don't discuss cures. Off and on during the past twenty years, I've tried to help numerous parents in this group, but most of them feel it futile to put in the hard work, don't believe in recovery, and don't see a need or much hope of getting their child to adapt to their world.

Over the past four decades, many neuropsychiatric conditions/illnesses have been added to the diagnostic definition of autism; so many, in fact, that autism had to become a spectrum, an encompassing line up of special needs children stepping under the umbrella of autism, including Cerebral Palsy, Down's Syndrome, ADHD, OCD, LD, and Asperger's Syndrome. These loosely share the revised basic defining characteristics/behaviors of autism but come with some completely dissimilar symptoms and causations... not to mention treatments. This group's autism umbrella is now so broad that everyone is confused about what autism itself is.

The general public knows what cerebral palsy is; they know and recognize Down's Syndrome, and OCD; after those, group one steps into some pretty cloudy puddles under their big umbrella.

The other group, the second, smaller group, I guess I could call the purists, and I am in this group. We clearly know what an autistic child is and we recognize them when we see them whether they be severe, moderate or slightly autistic. Most of the currently defined spectrum members don't belong under the autism umbrella at all. For example, I meet people all the time who say their child is autistic and yet their child drives, goes to college, has two-way conversations, and functions in regular classroom settings without a paraprofessional present. This is not the autistic child. This is someone with social limits, quirky, perhaps anti-social behaviors, and communications difficulties. At times, I can be observed acting somewhat like this.

Many in this second group, myself included, believe autism is a medical condition like NIDS, PANDAS, PANS, all autoimmune disorders that affect the gut. Gut infections, malfunctions, and diagnostically tested conditions exist because the immune system is compromised. This group may well embrace homeopathic endeavors, total engrossment in different avenues of research, new vitamins, new treatments, and it is totally committed to fighting for their children and relentlessly working their children's ABA program at home. Members of this group want to put in the hard work, believe in recovery, and are committed to helping their child adapt to the real world they will all live in as adults.

Recently, I've been involved with VAXXED, PANDAS/PANS groups. These groups believe in healing, recovery, hope, and research on the immune system.

I would like for EVERYONE to know that Patrick was diagnosed Severely Autistic. With ABA therapy, vitamins, chelation, and other medical trials, he tested as moving from severely, to moderately severe, to mildly autistic according to the older diagnostic standards before the umbrella opened to be so inclusive. Patrick can talk, has control over his social behaviors, and takes care of his basic needs.

He also inspired my book "If He Were Your Son." To me, a book about his triumphs and trials proves that one of his purposes in this world thus far is to help, inspire, and educate others.

"A friend is the one who comes in when the whole world has gone out." Old adage

A Note From Christie:

I have yet to try chelation. As a parent, you never stop trying things. You give everything a chance. As Katheryn mentioned, there are many support groups out there. I have yet to go in person because, as an empath, I often feel the pain of others and it drains me. I'm strong enough in my mind and heart to do so now. Don't wait too long, don't get wrapped up in the diagnosis. We are here to help you with research, guidance, and support should you need it.

Chapter 13

When Challenges Happen
By Melissa Mottern

A Real Mom:
Emotional, yet the rock. Tired, but keeps going.
Worried, but full of hope.
Impatient, yet patient.
Overwhelmed, but never quits.
Amazing, even though doubted.
Wonderful, even in the chaos.
Life changer, every single day.
- Rachel Martin FindingJoy.net

I used to keep an eye out for that old adage "Seven years of feast; seven years of famine." Over the years, I've experienced both and also some years with all tangled up twists. For seven years my husband and I had been trying to have a baby. Long, disappointing years rolled out one sad, disappointing month at a time. We prayed throughout those seven years to have a child, and we finally conceived Parker. Our seven years of famine were over, and we were so ready to do some major feasting. That was in 2010. In 2012, we were tossed into a full out twister that tossed our parenting into a tornado.

Call it Devastation Day.

There was a gathering at the table in Parker's pediatrician's office that July day when Parker was two. The doctor's lips were moving, but his words were a distant echo somewhere behind the whirling in my head. "Parker is severely autistic," swirled and bounced around between my ears over, and over again blocking out much of what else was said. It was like my entire world came crashing down. My clearest memory of Devastation Day is me sobbing in that room and the psychologist, social worker, and doctor all trying to comfort me and give us information about Parker's future and our family's future and what that would look like, but it is all a blur.

When we left, there was no talking in the car. I cried the entire way home.

Given all I have learned about Autism, looking back now on those first two years of Parker's life the signs were all there. As a baby he never slept, and this is still an issue, he didn't make eye contact, he didn't point or wave. He would line his toys up. He wasn't interested in interacting with other children, wouldn't answer to his name. He walked on tip toes and flapped his hands. However, as the prognosis on Devastation Day played out over the next five years, his first two years seem mild. "He not only is non-verbal, but he will never speak," the therapist had shared that day. And that, too, is playing out. He is non-verbal but definitely communicates in other ways. He's seven now and has learned sign language, the PECS system, and, in August of 2016 he received his communication device. I am his voice and his BIGGEST advocate. It has been a huge transition, but he works so hard at it.

Parker is so intelligent; he understands everything we tell him to do and can master 2-step directions. He knows all of his colors and his numbers 0-10. He is a whiz at puzzles and loves books, but his true passion is technology. He is a genius with his IPAD. He blows us away with everything he's able to complete and figure out by himself on it. And, he is MUCH faster than my husband and me!

From a young age, we purposely took Parker everywhere with us. Although loud noises were not his favorite thing, we had to get him over that or else we would have never been able to leave the house--EVER. So thankfully, Parker can pretty much go everywhere now and is great, most of the time.

Sometimes I wonder how we made it through to this point. But, I know how; it's a joint effort, for sure. My husband and I are always discussing research to determine what we can do to further his potential. I always make an extra effort to stay very close to Parker's teachers, so that we can have open communication and I can continue to work on things at home that he works on in the school setting. I take him to private speech (2x/week) and OT (1x/week). Parker does his part in all of that and other 'outings' as well. He goes to special needs private gymnastics class. He attends local events around the community and participates in Special Olympics. I simply must share that he is the sweetest child you will ever meet. He is very loving, always wanting to give hugs and kisses.

I know that Christian is sweet and loving as well. Whenever Christie and I visit, I try to give her the best advice I can. I encourage her to continue doing as much research as she can on Autism. Early intervention is key, get your child into therapies (OT, PT, Speech, Play, ABA, etc.) immediately; find out about all the local resources in your area associated with Autism and use them; reach out to other parents going through the same situations you are—they will be your sounding board and shoulder to cry on; and overall get a great support group of friends and family, because you will need it. Finally, don't feel ashamed if you need counseling or help from your family doctor to get through the anxiety/depression that also comes along with Autism; it all goes hand-in-hand.

The best I can say to anyone walking in the world of Autism is to do what you need to do to survive and take care of yourself first and foremost, so you can be an amazing parent to your child! Personally, I didn't know how strong I was until I had to be for my child! Finding a way into your child's world of Autism is extremely important. You have to try over, and over again to find a way to get inside and become a part of it or else they will shut you out completely. This works for us and may work for you: find an activity that they love to do, interact with them and push them out of their comfort zone. They will push back at first, but they will get through it and are likely to let you in. Just keep at it. Focus on your successes because challenges will keep coming. They have for us.

At this point in time, I'm discovering that services are very limited or slowly disappearing for the disabled population, especially as they get older. We are currently on a waiting list for ABA therapy because insurance is holding up the process. Since Parker is non-verbal, can get overstimulated quickly, and makes loud noises, I have had ignorant people approach and reproach me about it. We definitely need more acceptance and understanding throughout society of what exactly Autism is. On a very personal note, I tend to feel isolated when friends stop calling to invite us places or even to call to see how I am doing. So many people don't seem to know that Autism doesn't define an individual; it is just one single part of them, only one part of who Parker is.

My ultimate hope and wish is that our society can get a better understanding of all the characteristics that make up Autism so that there is a greater overall acceptance and inclusion in our world. Everyone deserves that. Everyone!

A Note From Christie:

Everyone has a different story. Hope is what it's all about and what we want to give to others. Help educate others. When you have a child with autism your whole life changes, as do the people around you. It's a lot to take in when any child gets a disability. If you educate your friends and family on what you're going through, you'll have a better chance to keep them in your life and to be supportive. Remember, the support is more important for your child than for you.

When I was ready to let the world know, I shared this post on FaceBook: My son has autism. I'm so jealous. He doesn't care how the world views him. He does exactly what he wants without fear. He's my biggest hero. He has taught me to be brave and face my fears.

Sharing your diagnosis with others will help you and them.
Christian has taught me to be brave. I've overcome many fears to be more like him. Little Christian is fearlessly unafraid to be himself.

Chapter 14

The Flutie Foundation

By Lisa Borges, Director of The Flutie Foundation

"If you've met one individual with autism, you've met one individual with autism."
Stephen M. Shore

Being and Becoming

Our goal is to build the capacity of organizations that are serving people with autism. We also want to convene like-minded organizations, families, and advocates for a bigger purpose and shared goals, to provide avenues of joint goals. We believe it is important to collaborate and work together as a community, a nation, and beyond.

The Flutie Foundation is primarily a grant maker and not a direct service provider. However, we partner with multiple organizations to create programs that serve people with autism and their families. We support a summer water sports program, provide SafetyNet Tracking devices for individuals with autism who wander, and we recently launched a social enterprise utilizing business principles to fulfill a social mission of employing adults with autism.

The goal of the Flutie Foundation is to help families affected by autism live life to the fullest. Through our programs and partnerships, we help people with autism get access to services, lead more active lifestyles, and grow toward adult independence.

As the Executive Director of The Doug Flutie Jr. Foundation I am responsible for the successful leadership and strategic development of the organization as well as the consistent achievement of its mission and financial objectives. That's the professional lingo for the "buck stops (and starts) with me." And it's a big buck, with about $1.5 million in annual revenue. Currently, the Foundation has seven employees and they are also my responsibility. Financing comes from multiple revenue sources including contributions, fundraising events, foundation grants and investment income. Last year alone, the Foundation served over 13,000 autistic children and adults. Financial need is considered if a family is to be awarded a Joey's Fund grant or to be able to participate in our AccesSport America.

Our Safe & Secure programs also consider a family's financial need, but there is no specific income level required.

We have an annual online grant process on our website for Joey's Fund. Parents can also apply online or speak with our Director of Community Partnerships & Family Supports to learn more about our AccesSport America and Safe & Secure Programs. Those two programs do have a limited geographic focus, which is defined in our grant guidelines.

Working with All Ages

We serve individuals with autism of all ages. Families are the cornerstone of the Doug Flutie Jr. Foundation and helping them live life to the fullest is our top priority. Each year, we continue to see the need for supports and services to grow for all ages and across the autism spectrum. We're committed to serving individuals with autism of all ages. With that in mind, providing families with the tools and support they need along the way continues to be our top priority.

Looking ahead, we will continue to identify partnerships that meet the needs of families and offer a chance to improve their quality of life. We will also find opportunities to bring families together for fun recreational activities and increase the capacity of the autism community as a whole through our annual Partner Summit and collaborative relationships. Finally, we plan to grow Flutie

Spectrum Enterprises by adding a second micro-enterprise that recognizes the skills and interests of the employees and creating a website directory of products available for purchase online made by entrepreneurs and small businesses employing adults with autism. This is exciting, break-through stuff!

I do experience successful parental interactions while working for the Foundation. A mom recently wrote a letter thanking us for providing financial assistance for her son Theodore to attend a speech and social skills, class. She says in that letter, *"We have seen amazing improvement in Theodore's speech over the last couple of years, but his social skills were still quite delayed. This grant helped us afford a second day a week with his speech therapist, during which he could bring a typical developing peer to practice his peer skills. He went from no eye contact with his peer and asking questions only to the therapist, to direct positive interaction with his peer. He is still working on it, but we are so excited about his progress. My husband and I are self-employed and have had some weeks where we have had to cancel Theodore's speech because we had to pay the bills. So, we cannot express how much your grant has helped us-so that this summer we never had to make the choice between paying the bills and helping our son."*

One young couple took the opportunity to form a friendship while their son was improving his coordination and social skills in an adaptive dance class funded by the Flutie Foundation. *"Being with other people who "get it" is priceless. You cannot imagine all of the wonderful information about services, clothes, camps and everything imaginable that is shared among the parents. Sometimes you come in stressed, tired and overwhelmed but always leave encouraged, uplifted and smiling."*

I would like to share a few results from our "Fun in the Sun" AccesSport America Program:

Over 70% of parents reported that they noticed a change in their child's overall fitness level from participating in *this program and 80% saw an increase in their child's self-confidence. One parent wrote, "This program is a huge part of our summer activities and helps Nick both physically and mentally."* Another one commented that *"My son benefited greatly from the one-on-one instruction and really enjoyed standup paddle boarding, and he has become very good at it."*

Working for Changes

We do have some concerns about the perception of autism in the world today. One concern is that people generally think of autism as a childhood disorder. However, these children with autism grow up to become adults with autism and at age 21 or 22 (depending on what state they live in); they are no longer entitled to educational services. Children aging out of the public-school system need support transitioning into adulthood. An estimated 90% of adults with ASD are unable to obtain employment. Thus, more services and supports are needed for adults to obtain employment, housing, transportation and health care as well as to integrate into the general community.

We do work with agencies at the state level. The Flutie Foundation works closely with Advocates for Autism of Massachusetts whose mission is to assure the human and civil rights of individuals of all ages across the entire Autism Spectrum and promotes the availability of essential supports so that they may live fully and enjoy the same opportunities as other citizens of the Commonwealth.

The goal is to educate individuals with ASD, their families and other AFAM members/supporters to be effective, vigorous agents of change.

While research is important, it is not the purpose of this Foundation. Our focus is on getting individuals with autism access to the services and supports they need to live life to the fullest.

Since a lot of our calls are from parents in MA who are looking for funding, we refer them to their local Autism Support Center and SPEDCHILDMASS for their calendar of events. http://www.spedchildmass.com/

Other resources we refer parents to are ACT Today for their quarterly funding cycle http://act-today.org/

And the Exceptional Lives website to sign up for their newsletter. http://exceptionallives.org/

Organization for Autism Research also has some great parent and teacher guides: https://researchautism.org/

I hope that by being part of this important book, we will help many families and that the Flutie Foundation will reach more deserving children and adults living with autism.

See more at *http://www.flutiefoundation.org*

A Note From Christie:

To you, dear reader, if you are looking to help but don't know how, please visit *http://flutiefoundation.org* and see how you can be of assistance. Some help with their expertise and others with their time. Others still, particularly those that would like to help in person but are many miles away, help with monetary donations.

One of the things Lisa wrote that jumped out at me is that people think of autism as a childhood illness. However, these autistic children grow into autistic adults! I love that the Flutie Foundation works with autistic people of all ages.

If you are in need of financial assistance, go to their site and apply for a grant. Take advantage of every opportunity to help your child. Raising a child with autism is not easy, I'm thankful for Lisa, the Flutie Foundation, and other such organizations that do so much to help our children live their lives to the fullest.

Chapter 15

Dr. Springer Shares His Thoughts

"I'm a visual thinker, not a language-based thinker. My brain is like Google Images."
Temple Grandin

A note from Christie about Dr. Springer

I have been blessed to have found many knowledgeable and competent doctors to help Christian. I would be remiss if I didn't include at least one in this book.

Dr. George Springer is a Naturpathic Medical Doctor as well as a Chiropractor. He's also Board Certified in Clinical Nutrition. He practices functional medicine which is a branch of medicine that identifies the actual CAUSE of health issues. He uses natural measures to bring them to balance.

He has been instrumental in helping me with Christian. I honestly don't know what I would have done if I had never gone to Lifeworks Wellness Center in Clearwater, FL and gotten Christian his expert care.

I hope this chapter helps you as much as he has helped me.

Dr. Springer – Q&A

As a doctor of note in the field of natural wellness, I'm often asked to give my insight on dealing with autistic children. Here are some of the most commonly asked questions and my best responses. I hope they help you to get a better understanding from a holistic perspective.

1. What is the single, largest, misconception people have of children with Autism?

The largest single misconception would be that there is little or no help for these children. This is likely true from the perspective of conventional medicine where they are focused on a "pill for every ill" as they are with virtually every other health condition under the current medical, Big Pharma healthcare paradigm.

From my perspective and experience, the hope for these children comes with taking a global, entire body approach to what is going on for them.

2. How can you treat the brain via the gut?

There are two parts to answer with the gut-brain connection.

First, every single neurotransmitter made by the brain for regulation of the brain is also made in the gut, and has a similar regulatory effect on the peripheral nervous system. For example, serotonin is a neurotransmitter that affects moods such as joy and sense of wellbeing. When it is low, people often feel sad/depressed and/or overwhelmed. 80% of the serotonin in the body is made in the gut and there are more serotonin receptors along the lining of the gut than there is in the brain. So, imbalances, such as leaky gut, in the digestive system affect the level of serotonin (and all other neurotransmitters made there) which can have a large impact on moods and expression of behavior.

Second, when the baby is developing the in-utero, the immune system of the body and the nervous system have their origins from the same embryological cells. So, from the very beginning, there is a very intimate connection between the immune and nervous systems. Since 80% of the immune system is in the gut, imbalances in the gut have direct and significant effect on the nervous system. This not only affects communication of the nervous system within the body but also with communication and behavior with the outside world.

3. What foods are good and which are bad?

There are only two foods I would truly label as "bad". The first is refined sugar and foods containing high levels of sugar. There are whole books written on the addictive, neurological, immunological, and negative behavioral consequences of frequent sugar consumption. The second group of foods I would label as "bad" are those created by companies like Monsanto that are being genetically modified by splicing a pesticide (Roundup) into the seed and therefore the plants we consume. They say they are safe for humans, however, increasing evidences shows they are not safe for the millions of bacterial living in our gastrointestinal system that play a major role in our food digestion and absorption as well as B vitamin production.

There are many books out there that try to identify a list of potentially offending foods and come up with dietary plans that target these foods to be removed. Typically, these are wheat, eggs, and dairy. When parents avoid these foods, and they do not necessarily see a difference in their child, they are quick to assume foods are not an issue. To the contrary, from my experience working with children on the spectrum, every one of them have had food sensitivities to a long list of foods that are often "good" foods. These sensitivities developed from a leaky gut that allowed larger food molecules to pass through the lining of the gut and become the target of their own immune system and its subsequent reaction to them with all the immune, nervous system, and behavioral issues noted above. (See: Doris Rapp, MD – her work from decades ago is a place to really understand the effects of food and environmental allergies on children's behavior.)

So, ANY "good" food can still be a potential offender for any given child – if it has gotten through the lining and programmed as an offender by the immune system. However, in general, whole, unprocessed, non-GMO, organic fruits, vegetables, nuts, and seeds could be classified as good along with free range, organic eggs. Fish, meat, and dairy have their own problems but can be eaten in moderation and as long as the fish are wild and the meat is grass fed and grass finished, and the dairy is organic and preferably raw.

4. Can parents expect their children to live "typical" lives? If so, how?

"Typical" may be a bit overrated... maybe we should just say they will have extraordinary lives. The real answer is that there should be no expectation of limitation, nor a typical life only excelling to the degree possible. Look at the example of Temple Grandin and what was accomplished by her mother who did not treat her as "disabled." I have had children who I worked with who, today, are living "typical" lives and others who have had their health, speech, and behavior profoundly affected, and a few who are healthier but remain in their own world. As a general rule, the younger I can see them the better the potential outcome.

5. Can you recount a particularly difficult client that you treated? A success story.

I will give you two:

Olivia came to me when she was 3 and for the first several months I worked on her, there was little evidence that she was aware of me even being in the room while I evaluated her response to what we were doing for her to balance her digestive, immune, and nervous systems. She was profoundly lost in her own world. Then, about three or four months into our care, I went to the waiting room to get the family for their visit and, as Olivia was walking by me as I held the door, she suddenly stopped and simply hugged my leg. That was nearly 15 years ago, and when last I had heard, Olivia was living a "typical" life without any evidence of where she was at one time.

Carly came to my office when she was 8 years old. She was very combative and non-communicative along with having regular seizures to complicate her autism. I remember it took her mother, uncle, and aunt to secure her on my table so that I could even examine her on her first visit. She went on a hunger strike to avoid the supplements we were trying to disguise in her food requiring me to come up with other alternatives to accomplish our goals. Within 6 months, her seizures went from weekly to one every four months and gladly laying on my table as I evaluated her progress. Within a year she was seizure free, and her behavior, language skills, communication, and progress at school had greatly accelerated. Carly just turned 18 and is still catching up educationally but is a happy, healthy young woman that has made remarkable strides.

6. What would you like to see medically going forward in the treatment of Autism?

I would like to see medicine treat Autism in a holistic fashion rather than dissecting and trying to compartmentalize Autism into neurological, psychological, or "another"-logical disorder with another set of prescription meds to simply "control" and manage the symptoms rather than developing therapies directed at balancing and "correcting" the causes of the "behavior" expressions we are seeing. Look at the gut... look at the diet... look at balancing the physiology of the body... of the child... and not treat them as a test tube to be filled with various pharma-logical concoctions.

   I would like for medicine/big pharma to put children ahead of profits and acknowledge the role of vaccines (especially the MMR) play as an actual causative factor in many cases of autism as determined by the CDC's own research – research that was fraudulently manipulated to show a different outcome which is now being brought into the light by a whistleblower connected with the research that has all of the data that confirmed an Autism – MMR vaccine connection. To TRULY and HONESTLY evaluate not only the safety of vaccines themselves for EVERYONE but especially the benefit to risk of some 60 vaccines (and all the toxins they contain) before the age of 6 for childhood diseases that are self-limiting and seldom life-threatening.

   I would like to see medicine be pre-conception advocates for the mother to make sure her digestive/immune systems are ideally functioning beyond whether they are symptomatic; to evaluate chemical, pesticide and heavy metal overloads in pre-conception mothers and to detoxify them prior to conception; to advocate for healthy lifestyles and diets (not the food pyramid) for women and men prior to conception and during pregnancy.

   I would like to see medicine be more patiently compassionate and less heroic, sterile and intervening with childbirth along with not viewing C-section as a "standard" method for delivery. Over the past decade, the number of C-sections performed have increased – so, has the rate of autism. Correlation does not mean causality – but may be worth a look considering thousands of children and families are being affected. Conventional wisdom may consider this a "crazy" suggestion. Then again, at one time in history, a physician was committed to a mental institution for suggesting physicians wash their hands prior to delivering children. His sacrifice went on to save countless lives.

7. How have Christian and Christie benefitted from your care?

This is likely better answered by Christie - but, perhaps, I can say I have benefited them most by opening the door to knowledge of the digestion and diet connections to autism along with the potential influence of vaccines on the immune and nervous systems of Christian. "Doctor" by definition means teacher – I try to live up to that definition with my patients... Christie has been a great student and now a teacher in her own right.

A Note From Christie:

Dr. Springer has been invaluable to Christian and me. His guidance regarding health, diet, healing the brain from the gut, G.I., and being a great source of wisdom have been life changing for Christian. I can't thank him nor recommend him enough!

PART III

Chapter: 16

Early and Late Signs of Autism

> *"Hope is the greatest thing for moms of autism. Hope is what gets us out of bed in the morning. I'm on a mission to tell parents that there is a way."* Jenny McCarthy

I feel strongly about helping parents who are just beginning this journey. Because I am only a few years into my learning, I want to share some of the early behaviors your child may exhibit. I wish I would have had a handy early watch list like what I am sharing here.

Signs of Early On-Set Autism

- Avoiding eye contact (looks near but not directly at another)
- Restless arms, legs, trunk, head, any or all in constant motion, often twitch/jerky-like, and looking uncomfortable, even in pain

- No spoken single words or limited vocabulary by first birthday
- Tip-toeing
- Lining up objects
- No spoken two-word phrases by second birthday
- Disinterested in others' play or talk
- Repetitive actions
- Easily frightened/frustrated by five senses stimulation especially in public places, leading to crying/screaming (meltdown), which cannot be comforted
- Stimming - Self-stimulation behaviors (repetition of movements, sounds, movement of objects, i.e. *"Rocking, hand-flapping, spinning, repetition of words and phrases, blinking, tapping, rubbing skin or fabrics, smelling objects (more common in autism than other developmental disabilities; aka Stereotypic Behaviors (engaged in to block-out an over-stimulating environment, trying to stimulate themselves, or can't think of other things to do, like pretend play)." Autism Research Institute: "Self-Stimulatory Behavior," by *Stephen M. Edelson, Ph.D.
- See also www.raisingchildren.net.au - This site details stimming as: "… blocking-out an over-stimulating environment, trying to stimulate themselves, or can't think of other things to do, like pretend play." Also, "watching an object spin, fluttering fingers near their eyes, flicking

switches, opening, and closing doors, chewing or mouthing objects, and listening to the same song or noise over and over."

- Rumblings: Verbal sounds other than words
- Bolting: Running from the room (needing to change the environment)
- Meltdowns: Temper tantrums (way beyond typical 'terrible two's' tantrums)

Late Onset Autism: Sudden, severe, and often overnight loss of established skills and behavior, ages 3-14.

Signs of Late Onset Autism

Many of the same symptoms and behaviors of Early On-Set also occur in Late On-Set. While the cause of Early On-Set Autism continues to spark differing opinions, Late On-Set adds the Strep virus into the mix. These are the PANDAS children. Strep frequently returns shortly after it is gone, perpetuating the autism behaviors.

VACS - VAXXED

I'm sure, many of you reading this book know more about autism than I do. I've only been learning about it for the last three years. Nevertheless, I felt compelled to start helping others as soon as I accepted what was happening. While you walk this journey with me, George, Brianna and Christian, I will be open, honest and helpful. I am one woman in your support system if you so choose.

One major issue that we are facing today is whether or not to vaccinate our children. For me, the jury is still out. You'll need to learn all you can on this issue so you can make an informed decision about your children and vaccines. Although school districts require vaccinations before a child attends school, there is an opting out form you can sign. If your child is showing signs of early onset autism or is diagnosed with autism, you may want to carefully weigh your options regarding vaccinations. (VACS).

The controversial film, "Vaxxed," attempted to tackle the subject but it was met with many obstacles.

While much of the scientific world supports existing vaccinations (VACS) for children, the movie "Vaxxed," that was originally scheduled for release at the Tribeca Film Festival in March 2016, takes an anti-VACS stance.

Andrew Wakefield, who vehemently opposes mandatory vaccinations for children, produced the film. In 1998, Wakefield published findings that attributed the combination of measles, mumps, and rubella (MMR) vaccines to an increase in autism in young children. Many people came on board and became followers of his movement to end vaccines.

Later, his findings were deemed grossly incorrect, and he was stripped of his medical license and completely discredited. Thus, ending his career as a medical doctor.

Oscar-winning actor, Robert De Niro, is a co-founder of the Tribeca Film Festival (TFF) and the father of an autistic child. He originally supported the acceptance of the film, "Vaxxed" into the festival and made this statement on the Today show in early 2016.

"I think the movie is something that people should see," he said. "There's a lot of information about things that are happening with the CDC, the pharmaceutical companies; there's a lot of things that are not said. I, as a parent of a child who has autism, I'm concerned. And I want to know the truth. I'm not anti-vaccine. I want safe vaccines."

He is also quoted as having said, "Grace and I have a child with autism, and we believe it is critical that all of the issues surrounding the causes of autism be openly discussed and examined. In the 15 years since the Tribeca Film Festival was founded, I have never asked for a film to be screened or gotten involved in the programming. However, this is very personal to me and my family and I want there to be a discussion, which is why we will be screening VAXXED. I am not personally endorsing the film, nor am I anti-vaccination; I am only providing the opportunity for a conversation around the issue."

Despite De Niro's initial statements and plans to include the film, it was ultimately rejected by the TFF. When the film was pulled from the TFF, there was much controversy and discussion. Many articles were written about why this had happened. Regardless of this setback, the film was later accepted for a premiere at the Angelika Film Center.

From: Deadline.com – March 2016

"Vaxxed: From Cover-Up To Catastrophe," will have its premiere at New York's Angelika Film Center in an exclusive engagement starting April 1, following the deselection of the film by the Tribeca Film Festival. TFF announced the doc as part of this year's festival but canceled after questions were raised about the film."

While the CDC strongly advocates for the world-wide use of the childhood vaccines that have eliminated many epidemics, it hasn't closed the door completely on new research regarding the vaccines.

For me, the jury is still out. You'll need to learn all you can on this issue so you can make an informed decision about your children and vaccines.

Chapter 17

My Action Plan for Parents

"I see the world differently. You would be amazed if you had my eyes."
- Calvin Nye, a seventeen-year-old with autism, 2006

At the top of my list for parents and caregivers facing life with an atypical child is to help get you out of denial of your child's disability as early as possible. This will only make life easier on you and will best help your child reach their full potential. No one wants to have to face this, but living in your own personal denial may eliminate the great advantages your child would have with early intervention. Early intervention is key. I can't stress enough how important it is for you to act quickly once you are close to admitting that something is not quite right about your child's development and/or behaviors.

Be proactive. Schedule and keep your appointments with your child's pediatrician and express your concerns. Ask about testing and any other help your pediatrician can suggest. As a parent, you will know when it is time to insist on action. Sometime between your child's first and second birthdays, "let's just wait and see" is no longer good enough. Be persistent and demand that early testing is scheduled and done!

Once any results suggest your child is on the autism spectrum or may well be on the spectrum, your work begins. First and foremost is putting together a team of professionals to work with you and your precious child. You will be your child's advocate and administrator in putting together a strong team for your child. You will also be a watch dog! If any of the team members just isn't going to work out for either you or your child, find a replacement immediately. The first speech therapist Christian had was wonderful. When she moved away, his second speech therapist just wasn't working out for us. I quickly researched to find another. This therapist is still on our team today and remains an amazing part of Christian's development.

No one will tell you putting together a team is easy, it isn't. Your persistence, dedication, and commitment to your advocacy are the glue that holds a team together. You are the team leader. So, here we go!

You will need three different teams. A team of therapists, doctors, and your support team:

1) Your Team of Therapists

1. ABA Therapist
2. Occupational Therapist
3. Speech Therapist
4. Physical Therapist

2) Your Team of Doctors:

1. Your child's pediatrician
2. Ear, Nose, & Throat Specialist
3. Allergist
4. Homeopathic
5. Neurologist
6. Pediatric Developmental
7. Pediatric gastroenterologist

We were well aware that Christian suffered from stomach and bowel issues. Testing with his GI at age one revealed many conditions. He had blood in his stool, low iron, Giardiasis, no bowel control, and bloated stomach. Giardiasis is defined by the CDC as "... A diarrheal disease caused by the microscopic parasite Giardia... that lives in the intestines and is passed in feces." And that was just the beginning of my GI research.

I spent hours online learning all I could about GI diseases. I went as far as to photograph the screens I found. I researched auto-immune diseases and read everything I could find about heavy metal toxins.

My inner warrior mom was arming herself for battle, and information was my ammunition.

Arm Yourself for the Battle Ahead

Not only are you about to embark on doctoral thesis type research, but you will invest more time and money than you planned. That's okay. It's essential, and you will find a way to handle both your time and money.

And did I mention gas? A typical week for your child meeting with team members will include three to four appointments. Your scheduling skills will rise to new heights. Gather up good tools to help you: white board lists in the kitchen where the whole family can see at a glance who is scheduled when; a calendar just for you on your smart phone or written in a daily calendar that fits in your purse or man bag; a notebook you carry to house your questions and/or specialists' comments or requests; a GPS that gets you where you need to be. If your car doesn't have a GPS, your phone does. If you have neither, use a map search and print out your directions. If you're not PC savvy, your local librarian or any office supply store print center employee will find and print your map. You may find a team member who comes to your home, but most will have a place where they have set up a therapy center with supplies and teaching material your child will be using.

3) Your Support Team

As you can see, being a Team builder and Team leader will be taxing. You will need a support team for yourself. Family members need to be involved as much as possible. You need them to help lift you up and pick you up when you are down. You don't have time to be down for long, so keep your support team informed and close at hand. Friends who love you will be quick to support you. It may be a girlfriend who will answer texts or a neighbor or grandma who runs over on short notice. It may be phone calls with your pastor or coffee with other moms. You will sense who wants to be in your support circle, but it is important that you ask them. People don't say yes to a personal request like this unless they know they can follow through. Assemble your platoon to march at your side.

Finally, seek and find a respite for yourself. It may be a healthy habit you already have, like biking, working out, or yoga. It may be taking a walk in a quiet park or sitting by the sea. It may be a relaxing bath or just five minutes of lying down. Choose something that's easy to do, quick to get to, and just for you alone. This is your refueling stop. You need to refuel to keep moving forward. It will seem all too easy to get caught up in a web of drama and depression. You won't help anyone, including yourself, if you wallow there. Feeling sorry for yourself is not helpful either and will actually bring you and your family and your supporters down. You will want to stand tall and march on!

Chapter 18

It Really Does Take a Village

"Children with autism develop all kinds of enthusiasms... perhaps focusing on one topic gives the child a sense of control, of predictability and security in a world that can be unpredictable and feel scary".
Barry M. Prizant

    I chose to share my vision for Christian toward the end of my story here because it is what fuels my path to our future. If any of you have seen a vision board or made one of your own, you know it's filled with pictures of what you want in your future. You need a mental vision of where you want to go with your child, how your child fares along the way, and a potential your child can realize.

    I have chosen to take my child by the hand and walk with him to and through all the hard work it takes to help his team help him. This is important and encompassing. Little by little, Christian progresses, demonstrates successes, and gains more and more comfort levels.

I also have a vision of how Christian can thrive at home, with his family and extended family. My vision sees our family dynamics being very typical and as normal as possible. Brianna is a happy, fun girl who loves her little brother. They both love swimming so arranging for them to play in a pool or at a beach together is part of helping them both thrive together in our family. They both also need alone time and special things to do with me and with George.

As I grew busier with Christian's routine, Brianna turned into a daddy's girl. That happened naturally and is not uncommon in the growth of a girl. She and I enjoy our girly moments together. She is a little mini me and likes dressing up, doing hair and nails, and singing and dancing. George also has 'guy' times with Christian. They play soccer and love going to the park. George is an avid weight lifter and teaching Christian work out techniques is not only fun for them and bonding, but it's good for both their bodies and ultimately their health. This is us thriving at home. Regardless of changing circumstances, we have established roles and relationships with Brianna and Christian that we can maintain.

My wonderful parents John and Judy Juliano, aka Poppy and Nanny, are amazing. Grandma's and Grandpa's are vital, too. They can have their own relationships with your children that will not only give your kids a break from you but will add a dimension to your children that only a grandparent can add. My mother, "Nanny," is an essential part of my support team and works with Christian as a part of his team. She demonstrates her love and commitment to us over, and over again. She comes over to our home at the drop of a hat. She has regular alone time with Christian. Since he was very tiny her ability to enjoy quiet play with him is surpassed by none. She is also my primary babysitter and the person I could least afford to be without. Her loving support has allowed me to be a better mother.

Unlike George and me who always wanted to act like teachers, she could just sit beside him and play with her toys while he played with his. It doesn't bother her that he often ignores her presence or doesn't respond to conversation. That behavior, a common one with autistic spectrum people, frustrates George and makes me sad and somehow personally hurt. These are reactions George and I have to fight; Nanny just loves being with him and always gives Christian the certainty that he is okay and his world is safe with Grandma.

My dad, John, a lifelong body builder, is my port in any storm; he is always there to support and uplift me. When he was younger, we spent quality gym time together on a regular basis. He was my inspiration and taught me to be strong. I'm his mini me. He is my go-to person to pick up my kids. I am and forever will be a Daddy's Girl.

My Aunt and Uncle, Louise and James Juliano, have been incredibly helpful in many things, including the writing of this book. Aunt Louise is a Reiki Master and shares great insights with us. We're family, meaning that although we don't speak as often as we'd probably like, when we do, we pick up right where we left off. She says that Christian is an Indigo Child, "a natural child in an unnatural world." Ancient peoples did a much better job understanding and accepting their Indigo Children than this modern world of science is doing. Their spiritual understanding and natural foods put them light years ahead of where we are today. I soak up all she shares with me so there is one more level upon which I can reach Christian.

George's parents, the late, wonderful Jamil and the vibrant Soultanee Maajoun, have always loved us and offered their help. My in-laws, Gaby Maajoun, Nina Maajoun, Valentina Maajoun, Pierre Maajoun, Mary Maajoun, Mary Berokadso, and Munjed Berokadso have also been tremendously supportive. Our entire extended family has been very loving, considerate and helpful.

They say you can't pick your family, but you can pick your friends. When you pick the right ones, they become like family. They are there through the good and bad.

Soha Haidar is the one who inspired me to write this book. I never would have written it if not for her. She had asked me what I wanted to do and once I told her my dream, she pushed me. She told me I had a bigger purpose in my life and has supported me every step of the way.

Renee Meritt Wirth, Lakeisha Broughton, Brian Lee, Krista Carlton, Lindsey Wells, Nicole Fiesta, Rob Wilson, and the late Bashar Salaman and others have been extremely supportive.

There's a quote I love that goes like this, "Your friends should motivate and inspire you. Your circle should be well rounded and supportive. Keep it tight. Quality over quantity, always."

My friends have been heaven sent.

You see, it takes a family village to maintain our family!

Chapter 19

My Vision for Christian

"My son has autism. I'm so jealous. He doesn't care how the world views him. He does exactly what he wants without fear. He's my biggest hero."- unknown

    The purpose of my vision is for Christian to reach his full potential. Along our path to his potential, my vision is to keep him safe and secure and loved. I see our home as his fortress. This is the place where he will always be accepted for who he is. In turn, he is constantly opening my eyes and my heart to the world around us. It's my vision, seen through his eyes. He brings depths of love and understanding out of me that I didn't know existed. The possibilities of my potential come from him. It is a vision path for both of our potentials.

    He teaches me so much. The possibilities for me are amazing because of Christian. The things I learn from him are changing me into a better person. Life with an autistic child teaches us to draw deeper from the fruits of the spirit: love, joy, peace, patience, kindness, goodness, and self-control. I need all these, and he helps me reach deeper and deeper into finding them and learning to use them. I am being and becoming a better me. I advocate for him, and he teaches me. This will happen for you, too, when you open your eyes and your heart to the potential of your autistic child.

He opens my eyes to a different world. The love I have for him shows me over, and over that, I can do more for this little person than I have ever done for anyone else. He is my beacon of light. He is my path to truer, deeper love and commitment in anything I do. He is my inspiration and my motivation. And he does all this so naturally. George, Brianna, and I are all better people because of this special child. And, we're healthier, too.

He is our natural Indigo Child.

His modern science diagnosis from his doctors is not final. Whether he's High Functioning Autistic, has PDD, Celiac Disease, Asperger's or SPD, it doesn't matter. He is my baby, my son. And the love I have for him makes me stop at nothing to help him succeed. I will never give up on him, ever.

This part of my vision is simple: make him comfortable, safe, and secure while helping him become a good a person. I know he's a genius and he owns my heart!

Chapter 20

I'm Just a Caring Mom

Trying to Help

"The key to my heart? My children!!!" - unknown

    You, who are reading my book this very moment, yes you; you may very well know much more about autism than I do. Again, I'm not an expert nor do I consider myself one. I'm just a caring mom who has only been learning about Autism for the past four years. Still, after my bout with depression and denial, I feel compelled to help. I traveled a dark, lonely road for a long time. I spent too much time of my life angry and feeling as if someone had perpetrated a crime against my innocent baby son.

I had serious doubts about writing this book. I mean, what do I know? I only know what I went through. I said as much to Soha. I'll never forget what she said to me, "Christie, you have to share your story, it can save someone's life. Besides, how much do you need to know in order to help someone?"

I hope you take those words to heart – how much do you need to know in order to help someone?

Your Go-To Mom

I wish for you all to learn from what I share. Like in all learning, take what you can use and leave the rest, until you're ready for more. And you will be. My wish is that you will open this book over, and over again. Dog-ear so many pages that the top of the book becomes an accordion! Get inspiration from the stories when you need inspiration. Study the information until you own it for yourself, memorize the acronyms as you need them. You will need them in order to be an efficient researcher and an informed team leader. This is important to remember!

I'm not perfect. I'm not the Poster Woman for mothers who have autistic children. I shouldn't be put on a pedestal. I'm deathly shy about speaking in groups. I'm not ultra-popular even in my own town. But I'm here to help.

I think being positive is a choice, a mindset. Positive energy is a powerful ally. To that end, I would like to invite you to join an uplifting Facebook group

– The Power of the Mind. Soha Haidar created the group in May 2016. I serve as an administrator to the group. To date, we have inspired over 800 people. Please join us there for motivation, inspiration, and a positive jolt of energy.

Where would I be without you?

I would like to end this book thanking the people who I couldn't live without. I know I mentioned members of my family in a previous chapter, but somehow, I don't feel what I wrote previously does justice to how I feel about them and for how much they've helped me.

Mom and Dad, I draw so much strength from you. I can never thank you enough for all your help.

Brianna, you inspire me. You're only ten years old, yet at times I find myself leaning on you! You're amazing. Christian may never tell you how grateful he is for the many, many things you've done to help him, but mommy sees it. I appreciate you for your willingness to give, give, and give. Stay special and share your smile every day of your life.

George, you're my rock. If I searched the entire world to find the absolute best father, I'd find you again! You are as honorable a man as I've ever met. I appreciate all the hard work you do to build Honest 1 Auto Care to serve our community as you do. Our lives aren't perfect, but we have been able to handle everything life has thrown at us and not only are we still standing, but we are swinging away... furiously.

When our children become happy, successful, educated, independent adults, know that it's because of the positive and uplifting mindset you have shaped within them.

And to you... Christian. Wow, I don't know what to say. A stream of emotions just poured out of me.

My special, little Christian. Thank you for being you. Mommy would never ever change her life because you have shaped it. I promise to protect you, nurture you, educate you, guide you, accompany you, and be there for you. Someone once told me, in an effort to comfort me, that one day you will be able to work at a grocery store; that got me so angry! "My son is going to be an engineer!" I shouted.

The world is yours. You're not alone. You've got Poppy, Nanny, Brianna, Daddy, Mommy, organizations, doctors, therapists, a whole bunch of other people who are on your side – too many to count. I look forward to seeing how you grow. I'll be with you every step of the way.

Lastly, to you – reader. I offer a special, personal invitation to meet Christian. I have a Facebook group called, Christian's Way. Join us. See his pictures. Follow along with his progress. And share your encouragement.

Should you have any questions, please reach out to me. I'll do what I can to help. If you'd like me to speak to your child over the phone, via the Internet, or to a group, I'll make myself available.

Thank you for allowing me to share with you. If

you've recently received the diagnosis that your child has autism, don't despair. Prepare yourself. I'll help. We have only just begun!

My Favorite Links

Some of these links were referenced as resources for this book.

http://www.aacandautism.com/references

https://www.autismspeaks.org/family-services/resource-guide

http://www.apa.org/topics/autism/index.aspx

http://shp.missouri.edu/vhct/case4108/references.htm

http://bdkmsw.umwblogs.org/references/ caution with this one; years were skipped http://www.lifescript.com/health/centers/kids_health/articles/autism.aspx many helpful links

https://robots4autism.com/?gclid=COLIxZ_Lu9MCFVc2gQodjHEECQ includes reading about Sesame Street's Milo & Julia

https://en.wikipedia.org/wiki/Autism_spectrum

And don't forget You Tube, Google, and Amazon use these to search for latest info available

http://www.parents.com/shop/all.html?s=autism helpful shopping site for autism related products for bed/bath, furniture, clothing, and toys

https://www.autismspeaks.org/what-autism/treatment includes helpful, interesting links for events, probiotics and newest info on autism proceed knowing this organization's philosophy does not always support newest trends/philosophy or facts

Acknowledgments

There are so many people I want to thank. It takes a village to raise a child and another one entirely to help the parents of an autistic child.

First and foremost, my family George, Brianna, and of course Christian.

My parents, John and Judy Juliano

My in-laws (George's parent's) Soultanee Maajoun and the late Jamil Maajoun

Uncle Jimmy and Aunt Louise Juliano

George's siblings – Gaby and Valentina Maajoun, Nina Maajoun, Pierre and Mary Maajoun, Munjed and Mary Berokadso

I also want to thank the rest of my family and the rest of George's family. There are too many of you to name and I would unintentionally miss someone. You are all so loving and accepting of me, Christian, and Brianna. We love being able to call you – Family.

Father John Kouki and the members of St. Athanasius Syriac Orthodox Church

The great folks at All Children's Out Patient Care, East Lake Pediatrics, the YMCA Kid Zone, Cypress Woods Elementary, the Seal Swim School, and the Flutie Foundation.

Dr. George Springer

Dr. George Jallo

Dr. Jose Ferreira

Dr. Condino

Katie Clark

Audrey Nadicksbernd

Jay Rackenwald

Lindsey Wells

Soha Haidar

Lakeisha Broughton

Renee Merritt Wirth

Brian Lee

Krista Carlton

Rob and Lisa Wilson

Cham Klaib

Nancy Assia

Vanessa Gonzalez

Devera Losson

Gigi Risolo

Lori Binko

Megan A. Widner

Nicole Festa

Sam Haddabah

Joel Clemons

Alex Salinas

Juan Viteri

The late Bashar Salaman – We miss you

Don Grady

Thomas Young

Lauren Lopedito

Chelsea Duverseau

Rose Chamoun

Kyle Kripps

Tyrone Lewis

Riffat Merchant

Warda Rose Gabro

Lexi Gabro

George & Carol Bassous

Teta Eli Bassous

John Cassella

Kadeem Aiken

Martha Wilson Core

Angela Cochran

Martha Martin

Katheryn Luker

Melissa Mottern

Lisa Borges

Last but not least, I'd like to thank the staff at The Ghost Publishing. Thank you Shirley Schirz, and Lil Barcaski. This is the first book I've written and would have been lost without your expertise, guidance, and editing.

If I forgot to mention any of my other good friends, you're in my heart.

About the Author

Originally from Staten Island, New York, Christie and her family – husband George, daughter Brianna, and son Christian, live in the Tampa Bay area. She is, first and foremost, a mother and a wife. The happiness of her family and helping her children become kind people is her top priority.

She is a preschool teacher at a popular Learning Center. It was there where she first found a passion for helping children.

When Christie isn't fulfilling her motherly and wifely duties, she can be found at her local MMA gym working on her boxing skills or at the Beach. She enjoys taking her children to the pool and on play dates.

She makes a concerted effort to surround herself with positive and ambitious people and to give positive energy to those she meets. She also enjoys her "girl time," when she can get it. Every Sunday is Family Fun Day.

Christie is an avid participator on social media. She is a moderator at the Power of the Mind – A

Facebook group for the power of the mind and positive thinking. It's an online place where you learn how to process negative thinking and turn negative situations into lessons and opportunities. As C.S. Lewis says – "We are what we believe!"

    Christie also administrates Christian's Way. Another Facebook group. In it, she posts updates about Christian. She strives to spread acceptance of autism. "Awareness of it is not enough!" Please add yourself as a member to Christian's Way and help share any research, diet, or therapy you find beneficial.